Inside SCIENCE

Climate Change Research

Other titles in the *Inside Science* series:

Gene Therapy Research
Renewable Energy Research
Space Research
Stem Cell Research
Vaccine Research

Climate Change Research

Charles George and Linda George

ReferencePoint Press®

San Diego, CA

© 2011 ReferencePoint Press, Inc.

For more information, contact:
ReferencePoint Press, Inc.
PO Box 27779
San Diego, CA 92198
www.ReferencePointPress.com

LIBRARY OF CONGRESS CATALOGING-IN-PUBLICATION DATA

George, Charles, 1949–
    Climate change research / by Charles George and Linda George.
      p. cm. — (Inside science)
    Includes bibliographical references and index.
    ISBN-13: 978-1-60152-128-6 (hardback)
    ISBN-10: 1-60152-128-6 (hardback)
    1. Climatic changes—Juvenile literature. I. George, Linda. II. Title.
    QC903.15.G46 2010
    551.6—dc22

                                                                        2009053704

9871

Contents

Foreword 6

Important Events in Climate Change 8

Introduction
Science in Action 10

Chapter One
What Is Climate Change? 15

Chapter Two
Reading Climate Change in the Earth 29

Chapter Three
Temperature and Precipitation 41

Chapter Four
Climate Models 53

Chapter Five
Climate Technology of the Future 64

Source Notes 77

Facts About Climate Change 81

Related Organizations 84

For Further Research 87

Index 89

Picture Credits 95

About the Authors 96

Foreword

I n 2008, when the Yale Project on Climate Change and the George Mason University Center for Climate Change Communication asked Americans, "Do you think that global warming is happening?" 71 percent of those polled—a significant majority—answered "yes." When the poll was repeated in 2010, only 57 percent of respondents said they believed that global warming was happening. Other recent polls have reported a similar shift in public opinion about climate change.

Although respected scientists and scientific organizations worldwide warn that a buildup of greenhouse gases, mainly caused by human activities, is bringing about potentially dangerous and long-term changes in Earth's climate, it appears that doubt is growing among the general public. What happened to bring about this change in attitude over such a short period of time? Climate change skeptics claim that scientists have greatly overstated the degree and the dangers of global warming. Others argue that powerful special interests are minimizing the problem for political gain. Unlike experiments conducted under strictly controlled conditions in a lab or petri dish, scientific theories, facts, and findings on such a critical topic as climate change are often subject to personal, political, and media bias—whether for good or for ill.

At its core, however, scientific research is not about politics or 30-second sound bites. Scientific research is about questions and measurable observations. Science is the process of discovery and the means for developing a better understanding of ourselves and the world around us. Science strives for facts and conclusions unencumbered by bias, distortion, and political sensibilities. Although sometimes the methods and motivations are flawed, science attempts to develop a body of knowledge that can guide decision makers, enhance daily life, and lay a foundation to aid future generations.

The relevance and the implications of scientific research are profound, as members of the National Academy of Sciences point out in the 2009 edition of *On Being a Scientist: A Guide to Responsible Conduct in Research:*

Some scientific results directly affect the health and well-being of individuals, as in the case of clinical trials or toxicological studies. Science also is used by policy makers and voters to make informed decisions on such pressing issues as climate change, stem cell research, and the mitigation of natural hazards. . . . And even when scientific results have no immediate applications—as when research reveals new information about the universe or the fundamental constituents of matter—new knowledge speaks to our sense of wonder and paves the way for future advances.

The *Inside Science* series provides students with a sense of the painstaking work that goes into scientific research—whether its focus is microscopic cells cultured in a lab or planets far beyond the solar system. Each book in the series examines how scientists work and where that work leads them. Sometimes, the results are positive. Such was the case for Edwin McClure, a once-active high school senior diagnosed with multiple sclerosis, a degenerative disease that leads to difficulties with coordination, speech, and mobility. Thanks to stem cell therapy, in 2009 a symptom-free McClure strode across a stage to accept his diploma from Virginia Commonwealth University. In some cases, cutting-edge experimental treatments fail with tragic results. This is what occurred in 1999 when 18-year-old Jesse Gelsinger, born with a rare liver disease, died four days after undergoing a newly developed gene therapy technique. Such failures may temporarily halt research, as happened in the Gelsinger case, to allow for investigation and revision. In this and other instances, however, research resumes, often with renewed determination to find answers and solve problems.

Through clear and vivid narrative, carefully selected anecdotes, and direct quotations each book in the *Inside Science* series reinforces the role of scientific research in advancing knowledge and creating a better world. By developing an understanding of science, the responsibilities of the scientist, and how scientific research affects society, today's students will be better prepared for the critical challenges that await them. As members of the National Academy of Sciences state: "The values on which science is based—including honesty, fairness, collegiality, and openness—serve as guides to action in everyday life as well as in research. These values have helped produce a scientific enterprise of unparalleled usefulness, productivity, and creativity. So long as these values are honored, science—and the society it serves—will prosper."

Important Events in Climate Change

1896

Swedish chemist Svante Arrhenius makes the first connection between levels of carbon dioxide (CO_2) in the atmosphere and the earth's temperature. He was the first to suggest that CO_2 emissions from the burning of fossil fuels would cause global warming.

1990

The first IPCC report says the world has been warming and future warming seems likely. Some scientists disagree.

1988

Intergovernmental Panel on Climate Change (IPCC) is established.

1900	1930	1960	1990

1950s

U.S. oceanographer Roger Revelle begins studying the interaction between CO_2 and the earth's oceans.

1976

Chlorofluorocarbons (CFCs), methane, and nitrous oxide are identified as greenhouse gases.

1982

Strong global warming since mid-1970s is reported, with 1981 the warmest year on record.

1991

Mount Pinatubo erupts in the Philippines, dropping global temperatures by approximately 1°F (between 0.5° and 0.6°C) because of aerosol particulates in the atmosphere blocking some of the solar radiation from reaching the earth's surface.

IMPORTANT EVENTS

1995
The second IPCC report detects a "signature" of human-caused greenhouse effect warming and declares that serious warming is likely in the coming century.

2006
A new generation of climate modeling is developed. The Flexible Modeling System incorporates weather, seasonal predictions, and human-made climate changes.

2007
The fourth IPCC report warns that serious effects of warming have become evident. The level of CO_2 in the atmosphere reaches 382 ppm. Mean global temperature (five-year average) is 58.1°F (14.5°C), the warmest in hundreds, perhaps thousands, of years.

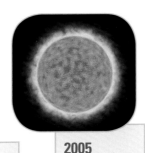

2001
The third IPCC report states boldly that global warming, unprecedented since the end of the last Ice Age, is very likely, with possible severe surprises for the future.

2005
2005 was the hottest year on record (as of 2010).

1995 **1998** **2001** **2004** **2007**

1997
The National Aeronautics and Space Administration launches the Tropical Rainfall Measuring Mission satellite, primarily for measuring precipitation in the tropics and subtropics.

2005
Kyoto treaty goes into effect, signed by all major industrial nations except the United States.

2008
The Jason-2 satellite is launched to measure sea level, wave heights, wind speed, and amounts of water vapor.

2009
The United Nations Climate Change Conference meets in Copenhagen, Denmark. The Copenhagen Accord, an agreement on reducing greenhouse gas emissions for the twenty-first century, is signed.

Science in Action

Climatologists—those who study the earth's climate—measure weather and climatic conditions and use those measurements to form conclusions about what the weather will be two days from now, two years from now, or two decades from now. Scientists who try to reconstruct the climate of the earth as it was in the ancient past are called paleoclimatologists. They study fossils, ice cores, tree rings, and soil samples to learn about the earth millions of years ago.

They believe, for example, that 3 million years ago in what is called the Pliocene epoch of earth's geologic history, the planet was similar in many ways to the way it is now, and yet different in others. Global geography—where the continents were located, for example—was very similar to today's geography. However, fossils found recently in the Arctic and Antarctic that date back to the Pliocene epoch show a much different world.

> ### climatologist
>
> A scientist who studies differences and changes in climate as well as how these affect life on earth.

In 1995 British geologist Jane Francis discovered fossilized wood and leaves from beech trees in Antarctica. The fossils were found only 310 miles (500km) from the South Pole, where the average temperature is currently -38.2°F (-39°C)—not exactly suitable for vegetation. Two years later in northern Greenland, Danish geologist Ole Bennike discovered fossilized Pliocene wood that came from pine and other cone-bearing trees. That area today is hundreds of miles north of the tree line—the northern edge of tree-bearing land. These discoveries, and the dating of the fossils that were found, tell scientists that the Arctic and the Antarctic were much warmer during the Pliocene epoch—warm enough for trees and shrubs to grow there.

A similar discovery in a deep, fossilized peat deposit on Ellesmere Island in far northern Canada tells a similar story. The area's climate has changed dramatically since the Pliocene epoch. In the peat, researchers Richard Tedford of the American Museum of Natural History and Richard Harington of the Canadian Museum of Nature discovered plant,

INTRODUCTION

10

insect, and mammalian fossils that suggest the area was once a grassy woodland of larch and birch. The site lies about 1,250 miles (2,000km) north of the tree line today, so winters then must have been much warmer than winters today.

Climatologists have been intrigued by these findings. Based on the fossil record, scientists theorize that the world's average temperature during the Pliocene was only 5.4°F (3°C) warmer than it is today, despite larger temperature differences in polar regions. These measurements tell scientists that if the average global temperature rose today by 5.4°F (3°C), our world's climate might be roughly the same as the climate of the Pliocene.

Additional measurements taken from the fossils found in Canada, Greenland, and Antarctica revealed that the amount of carbon dioxide (CO_2) in earth's atmosphere during the Pliocene was roughly 360 to 400 parts per million (ppm). Today the concentration of CO_2 in our atmosphere is about 385 ppm, and it is rising at a rate of about 2 ppm every year.

Paleoclimatologist Alan Haywood of the British Antarctic Survey says, "The concentration of CO_2 in the Pliocene atmosphere appears to have been almost identical to atmospheric concentrations today that are a result of the emission of greenhouse gases into the atmosphere."[1] Mark Lynas, author of *Six Degrees: Our Future on a Hotter Planet*, adds, "This suggests an obvious conclusion: If CO_2 concentrations at today's levels back in the Pliocene gave three degrees of global warming, surely they'll do the same now?"[2] This conclusion represents science in action in the study of climate change.

> **paleoclimatologist**
>
> A scientist who studies climatic conditions and their causes and effects in the geologic past, using evidence found in glacial deposits, fossils, and sediments.

A nonscientist might wonder what instruments are used to obtain this information and how they are used today to measure changes in climate. Scientists today use satellite technology, balloon borne sensors, deep-ocean submersibles, and numerous other devices to collect and analyze weather and climatic data. Without these instruments, scientists would be limited to only what they can observe firsthand and what is reported by others. It would also be impossible to reconstruct what the

Orbiting satellites are just one of the many instruments used by scientists for collecting and analyzing weather and climate information. With this information, scientists are able to measure changes in climate.

earth's climate was like millions of years ago, centuries ago, or even decades ago, as well as much harder to predict what the earth's climate might be like decades from now.

Where the Measurements Come From

During the past decade climate change has become one of the most controversial topics on earth. Increased awareness of its potential dangers has led millions worldwide to seek information about what is happening in the earth's atmosphere and whether or not documented evidence of global warming constitutes a crisis for every living thing on the planet. The majority of scientists believe that global warming is, indeed, a crisis and that it could mean enormous problems for humanity in the decades to come. A few scientists disagree that the problem constitutes a crisis but concede that the acceleration of global warming since the Industrial Revolution of the 1700s is due to human intervention in the earth's natural cycles of warming and cooling.

Virtually all scientists agree that humans are responsible for at least a significant percentage of the ever-increasing quantities of greenhouse gases being emitted into the atmosphere and the increased warming that occurs as a result of those emissions. That fact is not under dispute. What has caused heated controversy around the world is how to deal with global warming and whether or not it is dangerous for life on earth.

The question about what steps to take cannot be answered without hard evidence, and that comes from climate data—from precise measurements today and from records kept over hundreds of years by scientists and nonscientists. Current data is not always easy to collect. The accumulation of sufficient data can be accomplished only through the use of thousands of instruments, strategically placed on land, in the sea, in the atmosphere, and in space. New instruments using more-advanced technology come into use every day. Old systems are replaced with newer, more capable systems, which increase the amount and accuracy of climate data that can be observed and measured.

Once data has been gathered, scientists must decide what to do with it. After the invention of the computer, computations that might have taken weeks or months for a human

greenhouse gases

Any of the atmospheric gases that absorb infrared radiation produced by solar warming of the earth's surface, thus contributing to the greenhouse effect.

to complete could be done in a fraction of the time. Today's supercomputers can be programmed with massive amounts of climatic data, but the data itself would be no more than a collection of numbers without a precise computer program that uses mathematical formulas to analyze the data and answer questions put to it. Such a computer program is called a climate model, and it usually takes many models to assess the collected data and make predictions. Once these predictions are made, the results are compared or averaged to provide scientists with global trends.

Climatologists, meteorologists, and scientists in dozens of other fields have turned their focus to the creation of new methods of observing, measuring, and recording climatic data with a shared purpose. Their goal today is to determine whether global warming is a threat to life on earth, and if it is, what humanity can do about it.

What Is Climate Change?

The village of Shishmaref, Alaska, home to more than 500 people, is gradually being destroyed by climate change. The village, established in 1821, is located on Sarichef Island in the Chukchi Sea, north of the Bering Strait and 5 miles (8km) from mainland Alaska. The barrier island, a quarter of a mile (0.4km) wide and 3 miles (4.8km) long, is made of fine sand deposits held together by permafrost—ground that remains frozen for long periods of time. But the gradual warming of earth's climate is slowly melting the permafrost beneath Shishmaref, causing houses on the interior of the island to shift off their foundations and sometimes causing houses on the coast to slide into the sea.

The village plans to relocate southeast onto the mainland, to a place called Tin Creek. Even though the present village is small, it has been in existence for almost 200 years, and longtime residents are afraid this move may destroy their tight-knit community's unique identity. Their plea to the world: "We are worth saving!"[3] Melting of the permafrost is not limited to small villages in Alaska, though. Arctic ecosystems in the Northern Hemisphere are undergoing enormous changes, not due to changes in weather, but due to fundamental changes in earth's climate.

Climate and weather are sometimes thought to be the same, but they are different. Weather is whatever occurs on any given day—sunshine, rain, wind, hail, snow, or sleet, for example. The weather changes frequently, even when the climate does not change. Weather includes elements of wind speed and direction, temperature, humidity, atmospheric pressure, cloudiness, and precipitation. Occasionally, an area might experience a hotter-than-usual summer or a colder-than-usual winter, but these are weather variations and not climate changes.

Climate includes all types of weather that occur over very long periods of time. It includes a range of weather events that occur seasonally. *Climate* describes the "usual" weather of an area, rather than specific

Melting permafrost is destroying the village of Shismaref, Alaska, where houses such as this one have shifted off their foundations onto beaches, sometimes even sliding into the sea. Scientists say the warming of the earth's climate is to blame.

weather on specific days. Climate changes occur over hundreds, thousands, or even millions of years. According to Gavin Schmidt, a climate scientist at the National Aeronautics and Space Administration's (NASA) Goddard Institute for Space Studies:

> Climate, then, is the average condition of . . . environmental components over a period of time. . . . However, the average condition alone is not enough to define the climate. We also need a descrip-

tion of the variability over the same period—the frequencies of a cold winter or strong rainstorm, or the magnitude of the seasonal cycle—which is also part of a region's climate. The climate can be thought of as all the statistics of the weather (or of the sea ice, or the ocean, or the biosphere) but not the particular sequence of events in any one season or year.[4]

Why Climate Changes

Numerous events cause climate change, producing warmer or cooler cycles that influence everything that lives on earth. These changes are caused by various factors, many of them natural occurrences such as the movement of tectonic plates, volcanic eruptions, variations in the earth's orbit around the sun, the wobble of the earth on its axis, and solar radiation. Physicist Tim Hall, a professor at Columbia University, summarizes these changes:

> **biosphere**
>
> The portion of the earth and its atmosphere where living organisms can exist.

Climate is not static. It varies regionally and globally on time spans of decades to millions of years. Millions of years ago, dinosaurs lived on an Earth in which present-day Arctic regions were replete with subtropical trees and swamps. In the depths of the last ice age 20,000 years ago, much of now-temperate North America was covered with a mile-thick layer of ice. . . . As the Earth came out of the last ice age 11,000 years ago, it briefly—but suddenly—dipped back into a cold period that lasted a thousand years.[5]

Such factors continue to influence climate today. Scientists take them into account when they try to determine whether the current trend of excessive warming of the earth's surface—called global warming—is simply part of a long-term natural cycle, or whether the current cycle is being influenced by rapid increases in the world's human population and the industrialization that inevitably follows.

Plate Tectonics

The most basic of the natural cycles affecting earth's climate is the incredibly slow movement of tectonic plates that make up the earth's outer shell.

The Cartographic Division of *National Geographic* describes the movement of these plates:

> Like the pieces of a giant jigsaw puzzle, slabs of rocky crust known as tectonic plates fit together to form the Earth's outer shell. The puzzle changes as the plates slide over the hotter, softer rocks beneath them. Moving by mere inches annually, they reshape continents and ocean basins over millions of years by colliding, separating, and scraping past one another with relentless force.
>
> These interactions set off earthquakes, fire up volcanoes, and wrinkle the Earth's crust into mountains, valleys, and deep-sea trenches.[6]

tectonic plates

Large sections of the earth's crust that move against, alongside, or away from each other, causing earthquakes, volcanic activity, mountain building, and oceanic trench formation.

Plate tectonics contribute directly to gradual changes in earth's climate. One of the most dramatic effects of the movement of tectonic plates is volcanic activity, which can abruptly change a region's climate as well as have an effect on the world's climate.

During a single volcanic eruption, material from the depths of the earth moves rapidly to the surface and often is propelled high into the atmosphere with tremendous force. When eruptions occur repeatedly within a single century, the particulates—dust, rock, and ash—released into the atmosphere can prevent the light and heat of the sun from reaching plants and animals on the surface. This results in the cooling of the planet. If the sun's energy is blocked sufficiently for a long enough period of time, plants can die, destroying food sources for animals, which can die from starvation.

When more frequent or more cataclysmic eruptions occur, enough dust can be ejected into the atmosphere to cause the dying out of whole groups of plants and animals by blocking solar heat, leading to prolonged surface cooling and sometimes to mass extinctions of plant and animal spe-

particulates

Tiny particles of solid or liquid suspended in a gas. Some particulates occur naturally, coming from volcanoes, dust storms, fires, living vegetation, and sea spray. They are also caused by the burning of fossil fuels.

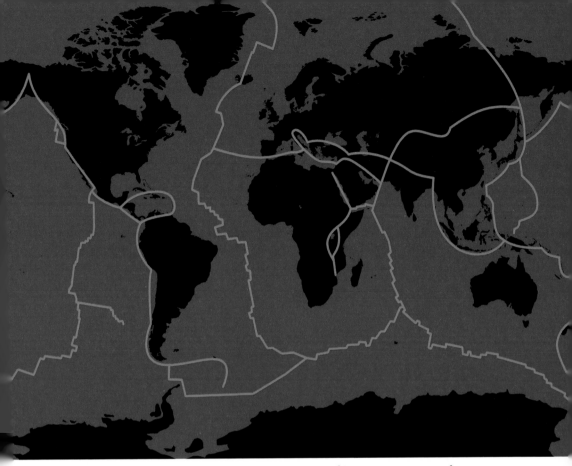

Red lines depict the boundaries between earth's main tectonic plates. Earthquakes and volcanoes are most likely to occur along these boundaries. The movement of tectonic plates can affect climate, both regionally and globally.

cies. These cataclysmic eruptions cause changes in climate that can last millions of years.

The most powerful eruption ever recorded on earth took place in April 1815 in Indonesia, off the coast of Southeast Asia. Tambora, a volcano on Sumbawa Island, erupted, ejecting particulates high into the atmosphere. The next year as a direct result of this volcanic eruption, most of the Northern Hemisphere recorded lower-than-usual temperatures during the summer months. In parts of Europe and in North America, 1816 was known as the "year without a summer."

More recently, the eruption of Mount Pinatubo in the Philippines on June 15, 1991, spewed an estimated 20 million tons (18.1 million metric tons) of sulfur dioxide and ash more than 12 miles (19.3km) into the atmosphere. For three weeks after the initial blast, gases and solids were propelled into the stratosphere, the second layer of earth's atmosphere that extends from an altitude of 6 miles (10km) to an altitude of 31 miles (50km). Within a year of the eruption, the aerosol cloud covered the planet, reducing global temperatures. In 1992 and 1993 the average temperature in the Northern Hemisphere cooled 0.7° to 0.9°F (0.4° to 0.5°C). The most drastic temperature changes occurred during the summer of 1992. According to Jason Wolfe of the NASA Earth Observatory:

stratosphere

Second layer of the earth's atmosphere, extending from the troposphere to the mesosphere and characterized by the presence of ozone gas in the ozone layer and by temperatures that rise slightly with altitude.

> Following eruptions, these aerosol particles [containing sulfuric acid] can linger as long as three to four years in the stratosphere.
> Major eruptions alter the Earth's radiative [heat] balance because volcanic aerosol clouds absorb terrestrial radiation [heat from landmasses], and scatter a significant amount of the incoming solar radiation . . . that can last from two to three years following a volcanic eruption.[7]

Surprisingly, after the Pinatubo eruption, winter temperatures were higher than anticipated, which did not seem to fit with the overall global cooling caused by the volcano. According to a study conducted by professors from Rutgers University and researchers from the Max Planck Institute for Meteorology: "The pattern of winter warming following [Pinatubo] is practically identical to a pattern of winter surface temperature change caused by global warming."[8] The researchers add that human-made emissions can worsen the consequences of volcanic eruptions on the global climate system. Normally, individual volcanic eruptions do not change the earth's climate, but exceptionally massive ones—or an unusually large number of eruptions within a short period of time—can.

A massive ash plume rises from Mount St. Helens volcano in this hand-colored photograph. The volcano, located in Washington State, erupted in 1980. Volcanic activity is one of the most dramatic effects of the movement of tectonic plates.

Earth's Orbit Around the Sun and Its Axial Tilt

Fluctuations in the earth's orbit and variations in how the earth spins on its axis also can have climatic effects. As the earth revolves around the sun each year, slight variations occur in the path it follows, changing the shape of its orbit from nearly a perfect circle to more of an oval. These fluctuations, which happen over 100,000 years, result in differing distances between the earth's surface and the sun. These slow changes, according to Tom O'Neill, writing for *National Geographic*, bring changes to the climate, as well: "Slow, predictable changes in Earth's movements have, up to now, been the primary cause of great climate shifts in the planet's history. Variations in Earth's orbit, tilt, and wobble . . . determine the amount of sunlight that hits Earth, setting long-term temperature."[9]

The tilt of the axis also varies slightly, because the earth tends to wobble on its axis in a process called precession that occurs over a period of approximately 20,000 to 30,000 years. These variations in axial rotation, combined with alterations in the earth's revolution around the sun, have affected the earth's climate. They have caused changes in the intensity of solar radiation that strikes the earth and warms it. Solar radiation is the planet's greatest source of surface heating.

Solar Radiation

Solar radiation consists of heat, visible light, and invisible forms of light. Visible light can be seen by the naked eye unaided. Infrared is invisible light that is responsible for the heat that sunlight carries to the earth's surface through the atmosphere. Ultraviolet light is also invisible and is generally harmful to living beings. The ozone layer in the stratosphere absorbs most of the sun's ultraviolet radiation, which can cause sunburn and even blindness if introduced directly into the eyes. Infrared is the part of solar radiation that is reflected back into the atmosphere from the surface of the earth. The heat from a glowing coal or an incandescent lightbulb comes from infrared rays. This heat can be trapped in the atmosphere, thus raising the temperature of the earth's surface.

The sun's radiation varies, depending upon several factors. One of these is variation in sunspot activity. Sunspots are dark patches that occur periodically on the surface of the sun—on its photosphere—that are so vast that 100

> ### photosphere
> The visible outer layer of a star, specifically the sun. This layer is where sunspots occur.

The Milankovitch Cycles

Milutin Milankovitch(1879–1958), a Serbian civil engineer and mathematician, advanced a theory that three regular cycles—in the earth's rotation on its axis and in the earth's orbit around the sun—affect earth's climate. The Milankovitch theory of climate change bases its conclusions on the measurement of those cycles—eccentricity, axial tilt, and precession. His theory allows scientists to predict long-range trends in climate change.

Eccentricity refers to the shape of the earth's orbit around the sun. During a cycle of approximately 100,000 years, the shape of the orbit changes from elliptical to less elliptical (more nearly round). These variations in orbit alter the amount of radiation received on the earth's surface.

Axial tilt refers to the "slant" of earth's axis. Because of axial tilt, the area around the equator receives approximately the same amount of solar radiation year round. But areas in the Northern and Southern hemispheres receive differing amounts of radiation, creating seasons.

Precession is the wobble of the earth on its axis, much like a top that is running down and no longer spinning evenly on its point. This wobble goes through a cycle of approximately 23,000 years, during which the axis points at the star Polaris at one end of the cycle and to the star Vega at the other end. Precession causes significant changes in climate. When the axis points toward Vega, the differences between summer and winter in the Northern Hemisphere are much greater than when the axis points toward Polaris. The earth's axis is currently pointing toward Polaris.

earths could fit across the diameter of one of them. They occur on the lower hemisphere of the sun and appear darker than the photosphere because they are cooler. Instead of 9,980°F (5,526°C), the standard temperature of the surface, sunspots are only about 6,740°F (3,727°C).

The area of the photosphere around a sunspot becomes hotter than it would normally be without the sunspot. This increase in the sun's surface temperature increases the amount of heat radiated to the earth. The more sunspots there are, the hotter the sun's radiation becomes. When sunspots are most numerous, scientists call that period a solar maximum, or solar max. When only a few sunspots appear, they call it a solar minimum, or solar min. One sunspot cycle goes from one solar min to the next. The sunspot cycle from 1986 to 1996 saw a change in the occurrence of sunspots from a minimum of 13 to a maximum of 157, and then to a minimum of 9 or less. In addition to the average 11-year sunspot cycles, there have been periods when the number of sunspots has been unusually low.

The most significant of these periods took place between 1645 and 1715, during the five-century period of extraordinarily low temperatures on earth often referred to as the Little Ice Age. Scientists have determined that during this period there were extremely few sunspots, and in some years there were none at all. This correspondence between the lower number of sunspots and colder climatic conditions led scientists to wonder if the two might be connected. If so, they also wondered how sunspots affect earth's climate during normal warming and cooling cycles.

More recently scientists have theorized that sunspot cycles affect earth's climate because the sun emits more radiation and stronger magnetic disturbances during times of solar max. This increase in radiation and magnetic disturbance introduces extra solar energy into earth's uppermost layers of atmosphere, causing climate changes on earth. George Fischer, a solar astronomer at the University of California at Berkeley, comments on the possible relationship between sunspots and climate: "One thing that is known for sure is that solar activity, which is what we call the general feature of having magnetic fields on the sun, changes the sun's luminosity—that is, how much energy is coming out of the sun—on the level of a few tenths of a percent. That could change the earth's climate in this cyclical way, but it's controversial."[10]

Some scientists believe the sun is the strongest influence on climate change, while others believe human activities, such as the burning of fossil fuels, the raising of livestock—which produce enormous quantities of methane, one of the primary greenhouse gases—and emissions from manufacturing are even more influential. But the correlation between the number of sunspots and colder climate conditions remains a compelling argument that sunspots influence climate by altering the amount of heat that radiates toward the earth. If heat from the sun was not retained near the surface of the earth, life could not exist.

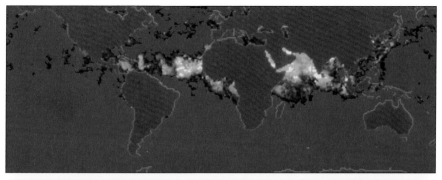

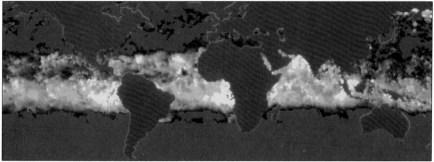

Global temperatures fell after the 1991 eruption of Mount Pinatubo in the Philippines. This illustration shows the distribution of volcanic gases and solids, or aerosols, in the atmosphere immediately after the volcano erupted (top) and two months later (bottom). Near-normal aerosol distribution is visible in the top image while a vast aerosol plume can be seen around the equator in the bottom image.

The Greenhouse Effect

Plants and animals—including people—are able to live on earth because of its atmosphere. Gases in the atmosphere nourish living things on earth in many ways. Some of these gases, called greenhouse gases, keep heat that radiates from the sun trapped near the earth's surface. The primary greenhouse gases are water vapor, carbon dioxide, and methane. Without greenhouse gases to absorb and trap heat in the atmosphere, it would escape into space, and the temperature on earth's surface would average 0°F (-18°C) instead of a livable average of 59°F (15°C). The process that enables these gases to trap and hold heat is called the greenhouse effect.

The greenhouse effect creates an envelope of moderate temperatures around the earth where plants, animals, and people can live comfortably. Greenhouse gases allow the sun's energy to pass through on its way to the

The Little Ice Age

Beginning sometime between the eleventh and thirteenth centuries and continuing until the mid-nineteenth century, Arctic pack ice advanced southward in the North Atlantic Ocean, glaciers expanded southward over land in the Northern Hemisphere, and temperatures were so unusually cold that the era became known as the Little Ice Age. The earliest recorded reference to this period came from the *Anglo-Saxon Chronicle*, published in England in 1046: "And in this same year after the 2nd of February came the severe winter with frost and snow and with all kinds of bad weather, so that there was no man alive who could remember so severe a winter as that, both through mortality of men and disease of cattle; both birds and fishes perished through the great cold and hunger."

During this period of intense cold, livestock perished, crops died, and many people froze to death. It caused periods of famine, a decline in population, a reduction in trade and travel, and an increase in rain, snow, sleet, and generally inclement weather. The much heavier snowfalls stayed on the ground for months longer than usual in many parts of the world. By the middle of the nineteenth century, though, temperatures began to rise. We are living today in the warming trend that followed the Little Ice Age.

Quoted in James Burke, *Connections*. New York: Little, Brown, 1978/1995, p. 157.

earth, but they prevent reflected energy in the form of infrared radiation from escaping back into space. Hall describes this process:

> Infrared [reflected] from the surface is absorbed by the greenhouse gases, heating up the atmosphere. The gases themselves radiate in all directions, including back to the ground and off into space, and this bouncing around of the heat energy keeps the surface warmer than it would be otherwise. . . . Greenhouse gases absorbing and emitting radiation keep heat energy in the lower atmosphere for a longer period before it ultimately escapes to space. . . . This is the greenhouse effect.[11]

In recent decades the greenhouse effect has been accelerated by the addition of abnormally large amounts of greenhouse gases. These gases have been emitted in extraordinarily high quantities since the beginning of the Industrial Revolution in the mid-eighteenth century. Increased use of combustion engines, growth in manufacturing, expansion of agriculture, and the raising of increasing numbers of food animals, among other factors, have overloaded the atmosphere—primarily with carbon dioxide and methane.

The greenhouse effect throughout earth's history has balanced the amount of heat entering the atmosphere with the amount of infrared radiation bouncing back into space. But in recent decades significantly increased emissions of greenhouse gases have accumulated in the atmosphere, where they have retained far more of the sun's heat than in natural warming cycles. The result has been an alarming trend that scientists call global warming. Their fear is that rapidly expanding and increasing human activities may be altering earth's climate in damaging ways.

Global Warming

Global warming is defined most simply as the increase of the average temperature of earth's surface above levels that would have occurred naturally if the Industrial Revolution had never happened. Since the end of the Little Ice Age in the mid-1800s, the earth's natural warming cycle has been measurably accelerated by the effects of industrialization—in particular by massive increases in the production of greenhouse gases. However, there are those who argue that this acceleration of greenhouse gas emissions and the subsequent warming of the atmosphere, though real, do not constitute a crisis. They contend that the earth is simply undergoing a natural warming cycle and that human intervention in the emission of greenhouse gases has not been significant enough to cause any real harm to the planet.

Most scientists, meteorologists, and climatologists disagree. The bulk of the world's scientific community believes the earth's natural cycles, when coupled with the acceleration of atmospheric warming brought on by humans, can lead to irreversible, damaging, and dangerous climatic changes during the remainder of the twenty-first century and beyond.

Which opinion is correct? How can we know for sure? The best way is to measure climate changes taking place today and compare those figures with historical records. Having done that for the past few decades, most scientists agree that changes in climate occurring today dangerously exceed the range of natural cycles. They also believe these abnormal changes may lead to climatic catastrophes that may alter humanity's way of life and its ability to thrive on earth.

Reading Climate Change in the Earth

Climate change cannot be measured without years, decades, or even centuries of accumulated data. Enormous amounts of data must be gathered, interpreted, cross-referenced, and compared. Scientists and experts in numerous fields can then study the data and formulate conclusions about how climate has changed and is continuing to change based on scientific fact, and not on speculation. To reach those conclusions, they study tree rings, sediment layers, coral rings, changes in the earth's sea levels, ice cores, and biomass—living and recently dead plant and animal matter.

Numerous types of measuring devices are used around the world to gather this data. They range from a simple thermometer to highly advanced satellite imagery and are placed on land, beneath the sea, in the atmosphere, and in space. Once gathered, the climatic data is analyzed by a vast network of scientists, representing disciplines ranging from oceanography to meteorology to geology—each of which approach the task from a different perspective. According to Stephen K. Ewings, author of *Global Warming: What You Can Do:*

> The annual averages of the global mean sea level . . . are based on reconstructed sea level fields . . . tide gauge measurements [and] satellite altimetry. . . By combining these three different approaches, scientists are able to build a clear picture of rising sea level that would not be possible if each was presented independently.[12]

Each of these disciplines focuses on climate data in different ways. Only a combination of all the data can produce an accurate picture of how climate has changed since measurements began and what the

---

biomass

The total mass of living matter that exists within a given environmental area, including all vegetation and animal life.

observed changes mean for the future of the planet. Studying instruments that scientists use to reconstruct climatic conditions of the past is important. It helps develop an understanding of long-term climatic changes. And seeing how they coordinate that historical data with measurements they take of current conditions helps develop an appreciation of how they can make predictions of earth's climate of the future.

> **altimetry**
>
> The science of measuring altitudes above a specific surface, such as sea level.

Biomass

Long-term or short-term changes in climate can produce dramatic alterations in habitat and availability of food, affecting how well plants and animals can survive in a particular ecosystem. In some cases animals adapt to changing climate by moving north or south to areas similar in climate to their previous habitat. When relocating is not possible, plants and animals may die because of climatic changes. Living plants and animals, along with their remains, make up biomass. Analyzing and measuring biomass helps scientists learn about climatic conditions hundreds or thousands of years ago.

Examining biomass and vegetation patterns in a particular region helps scientists determine whether climate change was a factor in the adaptation or destruction of a particular species. Instruments used in determining the changes evident in biomass include two components of MODIS (Moderate Resolution Imaging Spectroradiometer), a satellite payload launched by the National Aeronautics and Space Administration (NASA) in 1999 and again in 2002, to measure changes in the earth's oceans and vegetation. One of those components, the Rapid Response System, provides satellite imagery of the earth's landmasses, showing the effects of insect and disease damage to vegetation. The other component of MODIS is the Enhanced Vegetation Index, which maps density and changes in plant growth over a period of time. It also notes barren areas of rock, sand, snow, shrubs, grassland, and tropical rain forests, and evidence of desertification, where vegetation is gradually disappearing. MODIS scans the entire surface of the earth every one to two days. On-site soil testing can later verify satellite

> **desertification**
>
> The transformation of habitable (livable) land into desert, usually because of climatic changes.

imagery, providing biomass evidence of climate change within a specific environment.

One of the most important parts of analyzing biomass is investigating tropical forests, primarily because of the massive amount of stored carbon they contain. Mapping these forests is a huge challenge that has led the European Space Agency to launch the Tropisar airborne campaign. This ongoing project relies on an airborne radar system called SETHI. Each high-altitude pass over the rain forest generates about 500 gigabytes of data in the form of radar images. An estimated 3.5 million gigabytes of radar data had been collected before the project ended in September 2009.

⚛ Noah's Flood?

Some 7,500 years ago an enormous flood suddenly rushed from the Mediterranean Sea into the Black Sea. The rate of flow of floodwater was estimated to have been more than 130 times greater than the average rate at which water flows over Niagara Falls. Before this flood the Black Sea held freshwater. Afterward, it became larger and turned brackish (slightly salty and undrinkable).

Evidence of this massive flood has emerged from cores of sediment extracted from the bottom of the Black Sea by William Ryan and Walter Pitman of Columbia University's Lamont-Doherty Earth Observatory. Within the sediment cores, they found saltwater mollusks from the Mediterranean that they dated to 7,500 to 7,600 years ago. They believe the flood was caused by melting glaciers from the last ice age, about 10,000 years ago.

Sea levels rose dramatically, until the banks of the Mediterranean Sea could hold no more. For a time the Mediterranean overflowed its banks and flooded overland all the way to the Black Sea, adding a surface area the size of Florida to the sea's dimensions. The flood happened relatively quickly in geologic time, filling the Black Sea to its current size within only a year or two. Inhabitants of the region were forced to flee their homes and migrate into Europe. They took stories of the flood with them, and some historians think these stories may have been the seed of the Bible story of Noah and the flood.

When analysis by the French national aerospace research center is completed, project leaders hope Tropisar's data will help lay the groundwork for the proposed 2016 launch of the agency's seventh Earth Explorer satellite, which will include BIOMASS, a system that continuously observes the earth's forested areas. According to the European Space Agency: "The main objective of the BIOMASS mission is to provide consistent global estimates of forest biomass, its distribution and changes over time. In this manner, the mission is expected to greatly improve our knowledge of carbon stored in forests, and better quantify the carbon fluxes to and from the atmosphere from land."[13]

Tree Rings

Another method of gleaning climate change information from the earth is the examination of tree rings from trees that have lived hundreds of years. This is called dendrochronology. Trees add a layer of growth each year during the growing season, between older wood and bark. A wide ring indicates a wet season, while a narrow ring indicates a dry growing season. In addition to precipitation, the rings also provide information about temperature, cloud cover, and catastrophic events such as fires or volcanic eruptions.

dendrochronology

The study of climate changes and past events by comparing the successive annual growth rings of trees.

The data provided by dendrochronology is limited, however, because in temperate areas winter seasons are not represented in tree rings. The rings reflect only what has occurred during growing seasons. Also, trees in tropical regions grow year round and show no obvious annual growth rings, making their record difficult to analyze.

Keith Briffa, a scientist at the Climatic Research Unit of the University of East Anglia in Norwich, England, explains that tree rings—specifically their width and their density—provide data about changes in weather that occurred years before weather and climate measurements were routinely taken. However, he cautions that interpreting that data is not as easy as it may seem:

Tree growth is actually controlled by a complicated mix of climate-related factors. These include soil and air temperatures, soil moisture conditions, sunshine, wind, etc. . . . Ring growth

Growth rings, each of which marks one year of life, are visible in this cross section of a tree trunk. The rings provide a great deal of information to scientists who study climate change.

over a number of years is also affected by non-climate-related factors that include tree age, competition from other plants, soil fertility, attacks by herbivorous [plant-eating] insects and even changes in the composition of the atmosphere.[14]

Bristlecone pines, found in the western United States, are the longest-lived trees on earth. Some are more than 4,000 years old. Dead trees preserved in the arid climate of high elevations for hundreds or thousands of years provide a comparison to live bristlecone trees. Scientists can use their rings to construct a ring record that extends more than 9,000 years into the past. Tree rings from old Scots pine trees, which grow north of the Arctic Circle in northwestern Sweden, are another source of evidence of changes in summer temperatures that goes back hundreds of years.

Sediment

Just as trees record growth patterns in layered rings, layers of sediments at the bottom of lakes, ponds, and the ocean can provide data about climatic history. Each year, sediment is deposited in two layers known as varves. One layer composed of fine materials is topped by a second layer of coarser materials that contains organic matter such as algae and pollen. Varved sediment, when analyzed using biological, chemical, and mineralogical tests, yields specific data about environmental and climatic change.

> **varve**
>
> A layer or series of layers of sediment deposited in a body of still water over the course of one year.

National Geographic writer Virginia Morell describes the work of Cathy Whitlock, a fossil pollen expert and paleoclimatologist at the University of Oregon. Whitlock and her team extracted a sediment core from Oregon's Little Lake, using a lake-bed drilling rig. They then examined sections of it under a microscope, looking for pollen from thousands of years ago to determine changes in the area's plant life that would indicate a change in the area's climate. According to Morell:

In that pollen lie clues to one of the greatest puzzles facing researchers like Whitlock: What has caused—and will cause again—the sudden climate changes that our Earth periodically undergoes? . . . the more rapid shifts that scientists have recently identified when the Earth switched suddenly from frozen ice age to picnic-warm and back again. How often and how quickly have such dramatic changes happened? Perhaps most important, what do these past abrupt reversals tell us about the direction of Earth's climate today and in the future?[15]

The fact that scientists look for answers to incredibly difficult environmental and climatological questions in the mud at the bottom of lakes, ponds, and the ocean may sound strange to nonscientists. But the answers to big questions have often been found in out-of-the-way places or through the lens of a microscope.

Coral Rings

Similar to the record of climate change in tree rings and layers of sediment are the records found in coral rings. Corals, which can live hundreds of years, produce rings that exhibit climate change information.

Corals produce a calcium carbonate skeleton as they grow, adding rings (sometimes called growth bands) to the skeleton each year. The skeletons grow during summer and winter, with summer growth being denser. This difference in density is the result of differences in ocean temperature, nutrients, and the amount of light that reaches the coral. Coral rings also contain carbon molecules that record climatic conditions at the time the rings were created. Scientists are able to determine the differences in coral rings that correspond to rising seawater temperatures caused by global warming.

Much like tree rings, layers of sediment at the bottom of lakes, ponds, and oceans—called varves—can provide scientists with a year-by-year look at climate history. Varves, pictured, consist of two layers of sediment that can be tested and analyzed.

A study of Indian Ocean reefs has led to speculation that Australia may someday experience more severe and frequent droughts. The study, conducted by scientists at the Australian National University in Canberra, amassed a record of climate change and weather conditions going back to 1846 by looking at growth bands of corals. The corals told them that the Indian Ocean's tropical weather patterns have become more variable over the past century. Specifically, their research indicates that a regularly changing weather pattern in the region (similar to the El Niño/La Niña system in the Pacific that affects North American weather) has recently been cycling every four years instead of the 20-year cycle that it went through about a century ago.

Scientists reached this conclusion by examining growth bands of Porites corals found in the Seychelles, Bali, and Mentawai Islands. Just as tree rings can be used to reconstruct historic climate on land, corals' growth bands correspond to factors such as the temperature of the water, the level of salinity in that water, and the action of waves. This study allowed scientists to put together a climate history for the region that was surprisingly detailed.

Sea Level

Sea levels are changing around the world, and scientists are dedicated to finding out what natural and human-made changes mean for the future. All water expands when warmed and contracts when cooled. This expansion and contraction occurs seasonally, from summer to winter, affecting both sea level and ocean currents that move warm and cold water around the globe. As earth's oceans and atmosphere have warmed since the 1700s, sea levels have risen. This rise has occurred due to expansion, but also from the addition of freshwater from melting ice caps and glaciers, primarily in the Arctic. Scientists have determined that sea levels are currently rising at a rate of 0.12 inches (3mm) per year. One way of measuring rising sea levels is through the measurement of gravity on earth.

From 1992 to 2005 the TOPEX/Poseidon satellite provided daily measurements of sea levels. The Jason-1 satellite, launched late in 2001, measures sea levels every 10 days and orbits the earth in tandem with TOPEX/Poseidon. The Jason-2 satellite, launched in mid-2008, includes instruments that measure sea levels, wave heights, wind speed, and amounts

Death of Coral Reefs in the Galapagos

Since British naturalist Charles Darwin first studied wildlife on the Galapagos Islands off the western coast of South America and formulated his theories of evolution, the Galapagos have remained a unique location, home to such creatures as a seabird called the blue-footed booby, albatrosses, finches, penguins, giant tortoises, iguanas, and sea lions. The islands are a veritable zoological laboratory. Unfortunately, the islands are also one of the prime indicators of global warming. Their ecosystem is so fragile that the slightest change in climate has immediate effects on the islands' inhabitants. Higher temperatures worldwide caused by global warming are forcing Galapagos species to adapt—or die.

This is also the case for corals and their reefs near the islands. The fragile reefs are dying. According to German marine biologist Judith Denkinger, "The coral reefs create a habitat; they are like a forest, like the Amazon. They are home to scores of species. . . . If the corals die we lose thousands of species that are associated to the coral." She also says that pollution and climate change affecting the marine life could eventually cause the decline of onshore species, as well. "Everything is intertwined. You can't say this is land, this is sea, they are both one." The United Nations says that between 20 and 30 percent of plant and animal species worldwide are at risk of extinction due to global warming caused by greenhouse gas emissions. Island species are among those most vulnerable to climate change.

Quoted in Eduardo Garcia, "First Darwin, Now Global Warming Reaches Galapagos," Reuters, October 1, 2009. www.reuters.com.

of water vapor. Analysis of these measurements has led scientists to make a wide range of predictions for the rest of the twenty-first century. Estimates of how much higher sea levels will rise, given the current rate of global warming and the rate at which polar ice is melting, remain the topic of intense discussion. Most scientists expect at least 3.6°F (2°C) of warming, and possibly more, during the remainder of this century.

Stefan Rahmstorf, a scientist at Germany's Potsdam Institute and a widely recognized sea level expert, has come to some disturbing and controversial conclusions about what might happen to sea levels if the earth's average temperature rises 2.7°F (1.5°C). He believes that if such a rise takes place, sea levels may rise slightly more than 6.5 feet (2m). That would mean the disappearance of some island nations. His best guess is a 3.3-foot rise (1m) over the next 100 years. An increase of 5.4°F (3°C), Rahmstorf estimates, would cause sea levels to rise more than 16 feet (4.9m) over the next 300 years. He states: "There is nothing we can do to stop this unless we manage to cool the planet. That would require extracting the carbon dioxide from the atmosphere. There is no way of doing this on the sufficient scale known today."[16]

Another sea level expert, Pier Vellinga of Wageningen University in the Netherlands, concurs. Vellinga states: "Even if you reduce all the emissions in the world once this has started it may be unstoppable. I conclude that beyond 2 degrees [Celsius] global average temperature rise the probability of the Greenland ice sheet disintegrating is 50 percent or more. (That) will result in about 7 meters sea level rise, and the time frame is about 300–1,000 years."[17]

Ice Cores

Yet another method of measuring historic climatic conditions involves the extraction of cylinders of ancient ice, called ice cores. An ice core is a cylinder of ice that has been removed from an ice sheet by a hollow drill, taken to a laboratory, and examined under a microscope or using other scientific instruments. In polar regions snow and ice have accumulated for centuries, trapping air bubbles and creating a record of environmental factors. Most ice cores are taken from Antarctica, Greenland, or high mountain glaciers the world over, where snow and ice accumulations have been preserved the longest. The deeper the core is, the older the samples are, giving scientists a time line of climate, from the most recent at the top of the core to the oldest at the bottom. Ice cores can provide information covering a few years or hundreds of thousands of years of climate change. According to Ewings:

> Ice cores contain an abundance of climate information. Inclusions in the snow of each year remain in the ice, such as wind-blown dust, ash, bubbles or atmospheric gas and radioactive substances. . . . [They also provide information about] temperature, ocean volume, precipitation, chemistry and gas composition of the atmosphere near the Earth, volcanic eruptions, solar radiation, sea-surface productivity, desert extent and forest fires.[18]

A glaciologist extracts a cylindrical ice core obtained by drilling deep within the Antarctic ice sheet. By examining and analyzing the sample, scientists can develop a time line of changes in the earth's climate.

The deepest ice core ever studied was obtained during a joint project involving the United States and France at the Russian Vostok Station, near the South Geomagnetic Pole, at the center of the East Antarctic ice sheet. Drilling there reached an incredible depth of 2.25 miles (3.6km) in January 1998. The ice core taken from that depth was more than 400,000 years old. Other ice-drilling projects have included the Greenland Ice Core Project, which revealed rapid climate changes during the last glacial period (some 10,000 to 15,000 years ago); the North Greenland Ice Core Project, which was a multinational effort; and the West Antarctic Ice Sheet Divide, which was funded by the National Science Foundation.

These are only a few examples of how scientists have used measurements of historic climate records in the earth to formulate startling, controversial, and sometimes frightening predictions about what might happen if global warming is not addressed and if steps are not taken to slow the rate of greenhouse gas emissions into the atmosphere. Biomass, tree rings, sediment, coral rings, ice cores, and rising sea levels give scientists a picture of climate in the past. By comparing today's climate with what they have learned, a partial picture of future climate change can be constructed and used to help make more informed choices in the future.

Temperature and Precipitation

One of the most memorable events in the twentieth century involved dramatic changes in temperature and precipitation. It occurred during the decade of the 1930s in the south-central United States. For 10 years, one of the worst droughts in the nation's history hit the panhandles of Texas and Oklahoma, western Kansas, and the eastern portions of Colorado and New Mexico. This area was called the Dust Bowl. Powerful dust storms swept across the southern Great Plains, tearing away topsoil that had taken millennia to build. And this was while the country was still reeling from the Great Depression.

A 2009 PBS documentary, *Surviving the Dust Bowl,* provides stark images and reminiscences from people who lived through this harrowing time. The PBS Web site provides a written introduction to the film, providing a description of what the Dust Bowl was like:

> Crops withered and died. . . . The dust storms . . . rolled in without warning, blotting out the sun and casting entire towns into darkness. Afterward, there was dust everywhere—in food, in water, in the lungs of animals and people. . . . People tried to protect themselves by hanging wet sheets in front of doorways and windows to filter the dirt. They stuffed window frames with gummed tape and rags. But keeping the fine particles out was impossible. The dust permeated the tiniest cracks and crevices. . . . Animals were found dead in the fields, their stomachs coated with two inches of dirt. People spat up clods of dirt as big around as a pencil. An epidemic raged throughout the Plains: they called it dust pneumonia.[19]

During that dry, dusty decade, temperatures in the region often stayed above 100°F (37°C) for days or sometimes weeks at a time. Those who lived through those hot, dry days learned to treasure rain. Floyd Coen, a Kansas resident who survived the ordeal, describes what it was like in

CHAPTER THREE

41

1939, when the rains finally came: "It was a very emotional time, when you'd get rain, because it meant so much to you. You didn't have false hope then. When the rain came, it meant life itself. It meant a future."[20]

Moderate temperatures and enough precipitation to sustain plants, animals, and humans are some of life's most precious commodities. With the threat of global warming constantly in the news these days, it is important to understand how scientists monitor and measure temperature and rainfall all over the earth, because those measurements may tell us what can be expected for earth's climate in the decades to come.

Temperature

The simplest way to measure temperature is with a thermometer. Italian physicist, mathematician, astronomer, and philosopher Galileo Galilei invented the first thermometer in 1592. The basic design then—and now—included a fluid-filled hollow glass bulb attached to a stem with an imprinted scale. Traditionally, the liquid inside the thermometer is mercury. When the glass tube gets warm, the mercury inside the tube expands faster than the glass itself, causing the mercury to move upward in the tube. By comparing the height of the mercury to the scale on the stem, it is possible to determine the temperature of the air surrounding the glass tube. By including measurement scales on the stem—Fahrenheit, Celsius, or Kelvin, for example—it is possible to compare the temperature in the various scales. For example, 50°F is equal to 10°C and to 283.15°K.

Measuring the temperature in one location can be done fairly easily and does not require high-tech equipment. However, when scientists want to check up-to-the-minute changes in temperatures worldwide, they must use more than simple glass-tube thermometers that must be read individually by someone on-site.

Today computers gather temperature readings constantly from thousands of sensors scattered across the globe. Digital electronic devices called data loggers record real-time temperatures and transmit them by satellite to a temperature display on a computer. The Electronic Maximum-Minimum Temperature Sensor (MMTS) has largely replaced the traditional glass-tube thermometer because of its greater accuracy, even in climates where intense cold would break a glass tube. Tens of thousands of MMTS devices have been placed around the world, where they transmit temperature data to computers that analyze that data and chart it.

An ominous wall of dust looms over Stratford, Texas, in 1935. Strong winds eroded topsoil across the Great Plains in the 1930s, a result of poor agricultural practices and extreme drought.

To measure air temperature far above the earth's surface, scientists have long depended on radiosondes, balloonborne instrument platforms with the capability of transmitting their findings by radio to ground stations. These devices, in use since the 1930s, are launched twice a day from 70 stations across the United States and countless others around the world. Each radiosonde carries instruments that measure air temperature, humidity, and barometric pressure, up to an altitude of 18.6 miles (30km). Originally called a radio-meteorograph, the instrument got its name from a combination of *radio* and *sonde*, the Old English word for "messenger." A new and improved radiosonde, called a reference radiosonde, will improve the instruments' accuracy in measuring upper atmospheric humidity levels.

NASA provides other devices to monitor and measure climate data. One is their sensor web, a series of orbiting satellites that monitor numerous climate aspects, including temperature. NASA's airborne sciences division—a fleet of high-altitude research aircraft—also transmit climatic data. The most unusual of NASA's aircraft is the ER-2, a sleek research version of the famous U-2 spy plane from the 1960s. The ER-2 has long, narrow wings and flies at an altitude of 70,000 feet (21.3km). At that extreme altitude the plane's pilot must wear a pressurized spacesuit. Instruments on board the ER-2 measure, among other things, climatic temperature. NASA states:

> These high-altitude aircraft are used as platforms for investigations that cannot be accomplished by sensor platforms of the private sector. Aircraft and spacecraft have proven to be excellent platforms for remote and *in situ* [in place] sensing. The ER-2, flying at the edge of space, can scan shorelines, measure water levels, help fight forest fires, profile the atmosphere, assess flood damage, and sample the stratosphere.[21]

Seawater Temperature

MMTS, radiosondes, and ER-2 instruments measure air temperature, but there are equally sophisticated devices that measure the temperature of seawater. Argo, for example, is an array of free-drifting floats that measure the salinity, or salt content, of ocean water down to a depth of over 1 mile (1.6km), along with water temperature, currents, and surface winds. According to the Argo Project Office, Argo is

> a global array of profiling floats spaced . . . throughout the ice-free areas of the deep ocean. Together with a new generation of Jason radar satellites, the float array would for the first time systematically monitor the state of the global ocean (temperature, salinity, currents and winds) so that we could address the serious issues of climate variability and change.[22]

Argo floats were launched between 2000 and 2007. Currently there are about 3,300 floats in service. The floats spend most of their time in the ocean's depths. But every 10 days the floats rise to the surface in a journey that requires six hours, taking measurements along the way. When the floats surface, satellites locate them and receive their automatically transmitted data. The floats then sink into the ocean again to collect new data. Argo is a major contributor to the World Climate Research Programme's Climate Variability and Predictability Experiment project and to the Global Ocean Data Assimilation Experiment. The array is also part of the Global Climate Observing System/Global Ocean Observing System.

The use of remote thermometers, digital instrumentation, orbiting satellites, the ER-2 high altitude aircraft, and the Argo array gives scientists data on how both air and water temperatures are changing. Then current data is compared with data from the past to determine patterns that will help scientists predict future trends.

Precipitation

Precipitation around the world varies a great deal. Some places get a lot of rain, while others get little or none. The wettest place on the planet, for example, is Mount Waialeale on the Hawaiian island of Kauai. Its name means "rippling, overflowing waters," probably because one side of this mountain receives 450 to 500 inches (11.4 to 12.7 m) of rainfall every year. The other side of the mountain, in what climatologists

 The First Rain Gauge

Some say the first rain gauge was invented in 1441 during a period of extreme drought. Munjong, crown prince of the Choson dynasty in Korea, decided that digging into the earth to check rain levels was not as accurate as actually catching rain in a container to see how much rain had fallen. Munjong's father, King Sejong the Great, decided all villages should measure the precipitation that fell, in order to determine the potential harvest of each farm and thereby set the rate of taxation. Munjong sent identical rain gauges to every village so measurements would be accurate and comparable.

The Atacama Desert, sandwiched between mountain ranges in Chile and Peru, receives almost no precipitation. Because of this, the desert (pictured along with the foothills of the Andes Mountains) is said to be the driest place on earth.

call its rain shadow, receives much less precipitation. Conversely, the Atacama Desert, in southern Peru and northern Chile, is said to be the driest place on earth, because it is sandwiched between two mountain ranges—the Chilean Coastal Range on the west and the Andes on the east—that almost completely block precipitation from reaching it. This makes the Atacama the largest rain shadow desert in the world.

The average rainfall in the Chilean region of the desert is a mere 0.04 inches (1mm) per year. Evidence suggests that parts of the Atacama may have had no measurable rainfall from 1570 to 1971. According to Priit J. Vesilind, writing for *National Geographic*:

> **rain shadow**
>
> A dry area on the leeward, or downwind, side of a mountain or mountain range. The mountains block the passage of rain-producing clouds, effectively draining them of all moisture.

At its center, a place climatologists call absolute desert, the Atacama is known as the driest place on Earth. There are sterile, intimidating stretches where rain has never been recorded, at least as long as humans have measured it. You won't see a blade of grass or cactus stump, not a lizard, not a gnat. But you will see the remains of most everything left behind. The desert may be a heartless killer, but it's a sympathetic conservator. Without moisture, nothing rots. Everything turns into artifacts [or mummies].[23]

An essential element of earth's climate is precipitation, which can alter temperature through evaporation. Precipitation also provides the freshwater that living things require in order to stay alive. Precipitation includes rain, hail, snow, rime, hoarfrost, and fog, and all are measured using various types of rain gauges. There are two basic types of rain gauges—the nonrecording cylindrical container type and the automated recording weighing type.

The standard rain gauge—the nonrecording cylindrical container type that most people have in their yards—measures precipitation only near the ground and has to be read and emptied manually. Some cylindrical gauges have objects in them that float on the surface of the water, making them easier to read. Some cylindrical gauges measure amounts of snowfall. Ten inches (25.4cm) of snow usually equals 1 inch (2.5cm) of rain. Due to evaporation and other factors, however, these simple rain gauges are not very precise.

Automated electronic rain gauges are more accurate. They automatically collect precipitation, measure it, and empty themselves, and they are not affected by frost or freezing temperatures. These gauges use what is essentially a spoon or minibucket mounted beneath an opening that collects the rain. When rain falls into the spoon, it tips and empties once a specific amount of rain (usually 0.04 inches or 1mm) has collected. A magnet pulls the spoon back into place after it empties its contents, so the spoon is ready to collect more rainwater. The device records the number of times the spoon tips and empties, thus determining how much rain has fallen. Electronic rain gauges can also transmit rainfall totals to a computer that records and charts the data. Another name for this type of rain gauge is a tipping bucket.

Precipitation can also be measured using weather radar, satellites, disdrometers (instruments that measure drop size and velocity), and other instruments that use laser optics. Special weather radar systems locate precipitation, determine what type it is and where it is moving, and estimate rainfall amounts based on computer analysis. Weather satellites estimate rainfall amounts in much the same way.

A disdrometer uses microwave or laser technology to measure drop size and velocity. The new laser precipitation monitor uses a laser beam that is projected and reflected across an open area in its center. Changes in the beam indicate what type of precipitation is falling, how big the drops are, how hard they are falling, and how much they might interfere with visibility. Disdrometers and laser precipitation monitors are extremely accurate and precise.

> **disdrometer**
>
> An instrument used to measure the size and velocity of raindrops and hailstones.

Weather Radar

The radar displayed on daily weather reports finds rain, snow, or other precipitation, determines its movement, identifies its type and intensity, and forecasts where it will be over time. Most weather radar is Doppler radar, which also detects the movement of raindrops in addition to intensity. By analyzing how storms are structured, how much rain or other precipitation they are producing, the direction they are moving, and at what speed they are moving, people living in the path of the storm can learn what to expect before the storm reaches their position.

> ### Doppler radar
>
> A type of radar that detects movement within storms by measuring differences between movement toward and movement away from the receiver, allowing for the identification of tornadoes and other weather phenomena.

These measurements of precipitation can be recorded and compared with similar weather events of the past in order to determine whether the amount of precipitation in a particular area is increasing, decreasing, or becoming more or less intense. Such analysis can paint a picture of climate change based solely on the amount of water vapor reaching the earth through precipitation.

The Tropical Rainfall Measuring Mission

Weather satellites monitor weather and climate on earth, including clouds, cloud systems, fires, pollution, auroras, sand and dust storms, snow cover, ice caps, ocean currents, energy flow, and many other aspects of earth's climate. These satellites use two types of imaging—infrared and visible. Visible images are just what they sound like—images that can be seen and photographed by a black-and-white video camera. Infrared images measure the temperature of clouds, landmasses, or seawater.

The Tropical Rainfall Measuring Mission (TRMM), launched in 1997, is a joint project of NASA and Japan's National Space Development Agency (NASDA). The TRMM satellite primarily monitors the earth's tropical and subtropical regions. There are three primary instruments on the TRMM: the Precipitation Radar, the TRMM Microwave Imager, and the Visible and Infrared Scanner. The most innovative of these instruments is the Precipitation Radar, designed by NASDA. It provides 3-dimensional maps of the structure of storms, including the distribution of rain, the intensity of rainfall, the depth of the storm, and the elevation at which snow melts into rain, up to 12 miles (20km) above earth's surface. Ground weather stations and radar have been measuring rainfall for decades, but these ground sensors have not been able to measure rainfall over the ocean. The TRMM is designed to do exactly that in tropical and subtropical areas, where three-quarters of the earth's rainfall occurs.

The TRMM satellite is also able to measure where and how much rain forms inside a hurricane. Tall thunderclouds known as "hot towers" serve as indicators of the amount of heat in the hurricane. Water vapor releases heat as it condenses, so hot tower clouds indicate stronger hurricanes. An example of the use of the TRMM was when the satellite captured data in 2005 from a forming hurricane—Rita—that identified hot towers 11 miles (17.7km) high, indicating Rita was intensifying and would soon become a much stronger storm. Two days after this data was captured by the TRMM, Rita became a Category 4 hurricane and devastated the Gulf Coast of the United States. According to Laura Allen, writing for *Popular Science*, "Such predictions weren't possible before TRMM, because ground-based instruments lack the accuracy and range to do the job."[24]

The workhorse of the TRMM satellite is the TRMM Microwave Imager, which measures rainfall over a wide area—547 miles (878km)—gathering data that includes water vapor, cloud water, and rainfall intensity. The Microwave Imager is not new. Its design is based on the Special Sensor Microwave Imager, which has been used on U.S. Department of Defense meteorological satellites since 1987.

The third primary instrument aboard the TRMM is the Visible and Infrared Scanner. This scanner ties in TRMM measurements with measurements made by two other satellite systems known as the Polar-Orbiting Environmental Satellites and the Geostationary Operational Environmental Satellites. By combining data from all these sources, a much clearer picture of the water cycle on earth can be obtained for use in computer climate models.

Also on board the TRMM are the Clouds and the Earth's Radiant Energy System and the Lightning Imaging Sensor. These two systems study the energy exchange between earth and the sun, as well as the amount and intensity of lightning strikes in the tropics. As accurate as the instruments on the TRMM are, however, climatologists are eagerly awaiting an even more accurate measuring system, the Global Precipitation Measurement Project.

The Global Precipitation Measurement Project

The successor to the TRMM will be the Global Precipitation Measurement (GPM) Project, scheduled to be in place and operational by 2013.

Annual Rainfall Change by 2100

According to the International Panel of Climate Change computer climate models, by the end of the century there will be more rainfall in the higher latitudes and on the equator and drier conditions in subtropical zones, including Australia, southern Africa, the Mediterranean, the American Southwest, and parts of the Amazon region in South America. The rise in rainfall amounts will be caused by higher average temperatures worldwide from global warming. Warm air can hold more moisture than cooler air, which means more rainfall. As the Arctic and Antarctic regions get warmer, precipitation in those areas will also increase, accelerating the rate of melting of ice.

The primary satellite will contain two instruments, the GPM Microwave Imager and the Dual-Frequency Precipitation Radar, but will be connected to what project leaders call "a constellation of satellites." Each satellite will have its own measurement capabilities, providing measurements of rainfall, rainfall processes, and cloud dynamics at a very high level of precision.

The GPM will orbit at a higher altitude than the TRMM. It is anticipated that the GPM will provide substantial improvements, with more-frequent measurement of cloud structure and dynamics and of precipitation. The GPM Project will be able to gather precipitation measurements from around the globe every two to four hours. It will also provide measurements of light rain and frozen precipitation that the TRMM is currently unable to measure. According to Sarah De-Witt of NASA's Goddard Space Flight Center, "GPM will usher in a new generation of space-based observations of global precipitation, a key element of the Earth's climate and also the primary source of freshwater."[25] NASA's director of the Earth Science Division, Michael Frelich, adds: "GPM's global precipitation measurements will advance our abilities to monitor and accurately predict precipitation on a global basis."[26]

No matter what type of measuring device, instrumentation, or satellite data are used, scientists now have proof that the earth's temperature is rising faster and higher than it should be during a natural warming trend after the most recent glacial period—the Little Ice Age. By analyzing data from hundreds of years ago, it has become obvious that the earth is undergoing a steady increase in global temperatures, including significantly accelerated climate change since the beginning of the Industrial Revolution. The reason for this extraordinary rise in global temperatures is, according to the vast majority of the world's scientists, the creation of industrial, agricultural, and technological advances by humanity that produce extraordinary amounts of greenhouse gases.

Climate Models

In 1998, one of the hottest years on record, East Africans faced a much different environment than they expected. Normally, the short rainy season would have ended and the river floods would have subsided. Farmers would have been ready to raise crops and animals, and the yearly tourists would have been arriving to go on safaris to see exotic African animals. But 1998 was much different from years past. Heavy rains fell and went on and on, causing flooding in Kenya and Somalia. Villagers had to crowd livestock into small areas of dry land. Camels, cows, sheep, and goats died from violent fevers. People also were afflicted with illnesses that left some temporarily blind and others bleeding uncontrollably.

The disease affecting people and animals was Rift Valley fever, spread by virus-carrying mosquitoes. Usually, the fever was not a problem. But with standing water everywhere, mosquitoes flourished and fed on any living thing, spreading the disease. At least 89,000 people caught the disease. Two hundred died, even though the fever is not usually fatal to humans. Animals were hardest hit, though. Up to 90 percent of herd animals were lost, causing extreme hardships for the human population. It was the worst outbreak of Rift Valley fever in recorded history.

The cause of this terrible fever outbreak in East Africa had its origins on the other side of the globe, in the equatorial Pacific, because of a change in ocean currents and winds that began early in 1997. That change affected weather around the world. It was called El Niño. The term *El Niño* was first used by nineteenth-century Peruvian fishers to describe warmer-than-usual surface water that arrived off the west coast of South America in late December. *El Niño* means "the boy" in Spanish, referring to the Christ child. El Niño cycles occur every four to 12 years and affect weather patterns in the Western Hemisphere and around the globe.

According to Mark Lynas, author of *Six Degrees: Our Future on a Hotter Planet*: "The last 20 years have seen stronger and more frequent El Niños, with the 1997–1998 event the most powerful on record. . . . El Niño may not only become stronger, but it may become permanent, spelling disaster for human populations and ecosystems around the globe."[27] Lynas based his statements on predictions from computer climate models and from paleoclimatological evidence. The modeling studies to which he refers are studies done by climate models—computer programs used to predict the future of climate on earth.

Thanks to climate models, climatologists and meteorologists around the world are more prepared for El Niños of the future. Mark Cane and Stephen Zebiak of Columbia University's Lamont-Doherty Earth Observatory created a computer model specifically to analyze the elements of El Niño and how various weather conditions contributed to the event. Cane says, "The model wasn't started to make predictions but to see how El Niño works, but it seemed to do the right things, so we tried it out."[28]

> ### climate model
>
> A computer program that uses large amounts of weather or climatic data to simulate interactions of the atmosphere, oceans, land surfaces, and ice, used primarily to help predict future weather or climate conditions.

Their model accurately predicted when the next El Niño would begin—in 1986. In the 1990s the model predicted a string of El Niños. New models followed, and predictions became ever more accurate and precise.

Data for Climate Models

After gathering information from ice cores, tree rings, coral rings, temperatures, precipitation, and many other sources of past climate records, climatologists needed to come up with a way to combine the data so they could spot trends and changes and try to figure out what caused those changes. They wanted to be able to create a picture of climate throughout earth's history—in ancient times, in the past few thousand years, in the past few hundred years, in the past century, in the past few decades, and in the past few days and hours. Seeing changes that had already occurred could provide hints about ongoing climate change and would help them forecast changes yet to come.

According to the Environmental Protection Agency:

> The Earth's climate is very complex and involves the influences of air, land, and oceans on one another. Scientists use computer models to study these interactions. The models project future

climate changes based on expected changes to the atmosphere. Though the models are not exact, they are able to simulate many aspects of the climate. Scientists reason that if the models can mimic currently observed features of the climate, then they are also most likely able to project future changes.[29]

This process of gathering information and assimilating it—putting it together—could not be done without computers. A computer climate model is basically a computer software program that simulates climate by

⚛ Discerning the Future by Looking at the Past

"How do we know when the changes we see today signal a dangerous trajectory of ecological change?" asks Tony Barnosky, a professor of mammalian paleobiology at the University of California at Berkeley. Barnosky continues:

> One way to answer that question is to look to the past in order to learn what kinds of ecological changes can be considered "natural," and then to examine the changes we see today and identify which fall outside that range. The problem with actually doing that, however, is that it requires pulling together an immense amount of paleontological information—specifically, who lived where and when—that is needed to reconstruct past ecosystems, in order to understand how those ecosystems worked.

MIOMAP—the Miocene Mammal Mapping Project—is a Web-based resource, constructed by Barnosky, postdoctorate researcher Marc Carrasco, and several graduate students. It contains information about which mammals lived where in the United States throughout the past 30 million years. By learning how the various species of mammals developed, branched into other species, flourished, or declined, paleobiologists are able to link this progression to climate conditions throughout millions of years. This comparison helps with predictions of climate change in the future.

Tony Barnosky, "UCMP's MIOMAP: Mapping the Past to Forecast the Future," University of California Museum of Paleontology, January 2007. www.ucmp.berkeley.edu.

employing mathematical formulas to simulate complex variations in the atmosphere, under the oceans, and on land. Computer climate models analyze and predict things such as the effects of volcanic eruptions, the melting of ice caps, and the reflection of sunlight off the surface of the earth. Maria Setzer of the National Oceanic and Atmospheric Administration (NOAA) says: "Since we cannot recreate the Earth's atmosphere in a test tube in order to run experiments, scientists use computer-based simulations known as 'general-circulation models' to study the chemical, biological, and physical processes that drive climate."[30]

General circulation models follow the basic laws of science, such as conservation of mass (no mass is ever lost; it simply changes form), conservation of momentum (momentum is neither created nor destroyed; it is only changed through the action of forces), fluid motion (the movement of liquids and gases), and chemistry. These laws guide the computer models when combining climate data input from the oceans, atmosphere, and land, and changes in the energy balance caused by volcanic eruptions and fluctuations in the amount of energy from the sun.

hydrosphere

All of the earth's water, including surface water, groundwater, and water vapor in the atmosphere.

Climate models try to re-create and predict changes in the climate system, which includes the atmosphere, the hydrosphere (the earth's liquid water), the cryosphere (the earth's frozen water), the biosphere (living things), and the lithosphere (the earth's crust and mantle). By combining climatic factors, computer models approximate climate change of the past, duplicate current climate changes, and predict climate changes in the future, based on variables such as the estimated amount of greenhouse gases that are predicted to be released into the atmosphere.

cryosphere

All of the water on the surface, below the surface, and above the surface of the earth that is frozen or in a supercooled state. This includes snow cover, floating ice, permafrost, ice caps, ice sheets, hail, sleet, and seasonally frozen ground.

First Computer Model

The first computer climate model was created in the late 1960s by the NOAA's Geophysical Fluid Dynamics Laboratory (GFDL) in Princeton, New Jersey. The model's computer program combined information from atmospheric and oceanic processes and predicted how alterations in this

Heavy flooding caused by El Niño destroyed thousands of houses in Peru in 1998 and forced families such as this one to seek dry ground. El Niño cycles, which occur every four to 12 years, affect weather patterns in the Western Hemisphere and around the globe.

information could lead to climate change over a period of time. Before this computer model was created, scientists were limited to on-site observation and theories about what influenced climate change.

Joseph Smagorinsky, founder of the GFDL, felt that a new approach had to be taken to understand the fundamentals of climate change. This led to the first computer model. Smagorinsky felt that abrupt changes in factors such as the amount of greenhouse gases being emitted into the atmosphere could cause changes in climate that would not have happened naturally. But the data being collected was so extensive that a computer program was the only way to adequately combine, calculate, and compare all that data. That early computer, the Univac 1108 introduced in 1964, was state-of-the-art at the time, but it took up the whole floor of a building and actually could not do a fraction of what a desktop computer can do today. The Univac 1108 had only half a megabyte of memory, much less than most modern cell phones and MP3 players—a far cry from supercomputers in use today. According to the NOAA, "The modern supercomputer at NOAA's Geophysical Fluid Dynamics Laboratory (GFDL) currently provides more than 100,000 times the computing power of that early computer."[31]

Newer Models Analyze the Past, Too

Over the years improvements in computers have led to vastly improved computer climate models. In 2006 GFDL developed a new generation of climate modeling—the Flexible Modeling System. This model incorporates weather, seasonal predictions, and anthropogenic (human-made) climate changes. According to the NOAA,
"With this new system, GFDL scientists developed, and now are using, two world-class climate models that have significantly enhanced capabilities relative to the world's first revolutionary climate model that GFDL scientists ran over three decades ago."[32]

anthropogenic

Effects, processes, objects, or materials that are derived from human activity; human-made.

Using descendants of the original 1960s computer model, scientists are able to predict climate change of the future, but only to a degree, since some specific data on climatic factors still cannot be pinpointed at this time. Depending on variables introduced into the program, the models are able to predict numerous possibilities for the future of earth's climate. They are also able to reconstruct the climate of earth's ancient past more accurately.

By using the climate record in the earth itself—ice cores, tree rings, coral rings, and so on—scientists are able to identify similarities between climate records of the distant past, the recent past, and the present. For example, one model compares the Permian period (299 million to 251 million years ago) or the Mesozoic period (251 million to 65.5 million years ago) with climate information of the recent past and that of the present. In this model the mid-Holocene optimum (5,000 to 6,000 years ago) is compared with data from the year 2000, the last interglacial period (125,000 to 130,000 years ago) is compared with predictions about

2025, and the Pliocene epoch (3 million to 4 million years ago) is compared with predictions for 2050.

Carbon dioxide levels present in the atmosphere during those past times match levels in the year 2000 and projected levels for 2025 and 2050. By comparing the amounts of carbon dioxide, methane, and other greenhouse gases in the atmosphere today with the amounts present in ancient times, scientists can conclude that changes that occurred long ago could conceivably occur in the future.

⚛ How Accurate Are the Models?

Climate models can come close to simulating the climate of ancient times, but they cannot produce results that are more accurate than the data used to generate the simulation. For this reason, climatologists strive to provide models with the most accurate information, verified by multiple readings, in order to achieve the best results from the model. However, some critics contend that the earth's climate is too complex for today's climate models to simulate every detail accurately, and therefore should not be relied upon.

Journalist and environmental activist Mark Lynas illustrates the limitations of computer models:

> Climate models, by their very nature, are . . . picking apart the different bits of the climate system and trying to understand and describe them individually using physical equations. Put these equations together, the logic goes, representing everything from clouds to sea ice, and you get your model. But the whole of a complex and interacting system is not necessarily just a sum of all the parts. In a crude comparison, that is why doctors cannot reassemble a fully functioning human body by sewing together skin, ears, teeth, blood, nerves, and bones from a dissected human donor. The secret lies in the way all human chemical and biological components interact within a living organism. The same is true for the planetary "organism."

Mark Lynas, *Six Degrees: Our Future on a Hotter Planet*. Washington, DC: National Geographic Society, 2008, p. 274.

Manipulating the Model Data

When predicting the climate of the future, predictions must be centered on a question to be answered. An example might be, What can we expect if emissions of carbon dioxide continue at the current rate? Or, perhaps, Will the Arctic ice cap disappear completely if the average temperature of the earth rises by 5.4°F (3°C)? The NOAA's Maria Setzer explains:

> [Models] allow us to determine the distinct influence of different climate features. Changes can be made to one feature in a climate model, such as warming or cooling ocean surface temperatures, to see how those changes impact climate. Today's complex climate models are used to investigate the extent to which observed climate changes may be due to natural causes or may be attributable to human activities.[33]

By programming a general circulation model with an increase of, for example, 5.4°F (3°C), scientists can see from the model what can be expected on earth at that elevated temperature. According to Lynas:

> In the Arctic itself, model simulations suggest that 80 percent of the sea ice will have already been lost as the world approaches three degrees [Celsius warmer than the current average temperature] with only a small patch hanging on between the pole and the north coast of Greenland. . . . Most [current] models show an Arctic that warms much more slowly than is already happening in the real world: One [2008] analysis showed that sea-ice declines are currently 30 years ahead of those projected in the IPCC's [Intergovernmental Panel on Climate Change] models.[34]

This discrepancy between the model's representation and the actual conditions on earth raises the question, How accurate are climate models?

Filipino farmers plow their rice fields against a backdrop of smoke and ash spewing from the Mount Pinatubo volcano. Data from significant climatic events such as the 1991 eruption of Mount Pinatubo can help scientists test their climate models.

Accuracy of Climate Models

Climatologists know, based on climate records of the past thousand years and on written descriptions of significant historical and climatic events, exactly what happened and when it happened. Examples of these events are the Little Ice Age and the eruptions of volcanoes like Mount Vesuvius in Italy and Mount Pinatubo in the Philippines. Scientists test climate models by programming the model with climate data from a known event—such as the cataclysmic eruption of Pinatubo in 1991— then running the model to see if it re-creates, or mimics, the climate that actually existed. In this way the accuracy of the models can be fine-tuned. Models can also be tested by programming them with current climate and weather data, then comparing the model's representation of weather events with actual events occurring now.

About 50 national and international models have been developed over the past 20 years at various major climate research centers located in China, Russia, Australia, Canada, France, Korea, Great Britain, Germany, and the United States. In recent years the IPCC has consolidated data generated by numerous computer models into a more complex "supermodel." This consolidation, or coupling, is required because no computer on earth has the capacity to analyze all the data at one time, so coupled models are the only way to achieve greater accuracy, and therefore more confidence, in predictions. According to Thomas Reichler of the Department of Meteorology at the University of Utah:

> Coupled models are becoming increasingly reliable tools for understanding climate and climate change, and the best models are now capable of simulating present-day climate with accuracy approaching conventional atmospheric observations. We can now place a much higher level of confidence in model-based projections of climate change than in the past.[35]

Despite intergovernmental cooperation on computer climate modeling, environmentalists, scientists, and politicians constantly debate the accuracy of those models and the predictions they make. Some defend the accuracy of current models, as a recent article in *Science Daily* describes: "A new study by meteorologists at the University of Utah shows that current climate models are quite accurate and can be valuable tools for those seeking solutions on reversing global warming trends. Most of these models project a global warming trend that amounts to about 7 degrees Fahrenheit over the next 100 years."[36]

Other scientists disagree about the accuracy of climate models. Scientists from the University of Rochester, the University of Alabama in Huntsville, and the University of Virginia compared the composite predictions from 22 of the most widely cited computer models with actual data of the temperature in the tropics that had been collected from surface, satellite, and balloonborne sensors. The ability of the models to re-create the climatic trends that happened in reality was not very good, according to the group's report. The models consistently forecast that the lower atmosphere should warm significantly more than it did. According to Fred Singer from the University of Virginia: "The last 25 years constitute a period of more complete and accurate observations, and more realistic modeling efforts. Nonetheless, the models are seen to disagree with the observations. We suggest, therefore, that projections of future climate based on these models should be viewed with much caution."[37]

Whether defending or criticizing the accuracy of current-generation computer climate models, all climatologists understand that climate models are only as accurate as the data programmed into them and as the mathematical formulas provided for the model to use in analyzing the data. Hopefully, technologies on the horizon will do what they do not seem to be able to do today—provide predictions about future climate change that all climatologists, meteorologists, and environmentalists can agree on.

Climate Technology of the Future

For decades scientists have been striving to understand, describe, and simulate earth's climate in an attempt to achieve better forecasting techniques to prepare for future climate change. This process of fine-tuning the current knowledge of how earth's systems work together and affect each other requires constant diligence because the environment is continually changing. One international organization is trying to coordinate information from 28 space agencies and another 20 national and international organizations. The Committee on Earth Observation Satellites (CEOS), established in 1984, hopes to improve the measurement, analysis, and prediction of climate change in the future.

CEOS agencies know that more advanced versions of existing technologies, as well as totally new technologies, will be needed to answer the complicated questions surrounding global warming and its potential threat to humanity. On its Web site the CEOS discusses the importance of improving climatic observation, both short-term and long-term, and of better coordinating the activities of the world's scientific agencies in the future. According to the CEOS, analysis of short-term readings (accurate observations taken over days or hours) helps to improve weather forecasting and "to support operational applications (e.g. air quality, oceanography, land management, meteorology, disaster management)." Analysis of long-term observations (those taken over decades), the CEOS explains, helps "detect climate change and . . . determine the rate of change. Furthermore, this information is analysed to assist in attributing the causes of change; identify any anthropogenic [human] contribution to climate change; validate and calibrate climate models and assist in prediction of the future climate."[38]

These observations will do more than merely aid climatologists in creating more accurate climate models. The information they gather will be of immense help on a day-to-day basis for the people of the world whose lives can be instantly and irrevocably changed by weather events

CHAPTER FIVE

such as tornadoes, hurricanes, and tsunamis. The more information that is available to scientists, the greater the warning times for those people living in the path of severe weather. Climate observation is not only for the future. It applies to everyday life on earth.

The NOAA's Plan for the Future

The National Oceanic and Atmospheric Administration (NOAA) has an extensive plan for the next 20 years to improve and enhance their ongoing goals. According to NOAA researchers, long-term climate efforts will center on improving their understanding of the variations that take place in

Improved climate observation techniques will help scientists assess future climatic changes. Such improvements will also get better information to people who may be affected by dangerous weather events such as tornadoes.

Essential Climate Variables

The Global Climate Observing System (GCOS), an international institution sponsored by the World Meteorological Organization, various United Nations agencies, and the International Council for Science, has listed the environmental factors they consider the essential climate variables. These include elements in the atmosphere, on land, and in the oceans that need to be monitored and measured to detect climate change.

In the atmosphere the GCOS lists both surface and upper atmospheric air temperature, air pressure, wind speed, wind direction, and water vapor. The institution also lists radiation readings, cloud properties, precipitation, and measurement of the components of the atmosphere—carbon dioxide, methane, ozone, and other greenhouse gases. In earth's oceans essential climate variables include temperature and salinity levels, sea ice, currents, carbon levels, phytoplankton levels, and ocean color. (Color is monitored for changes in biological activity.) On land the GCOS monitors a multitude of climatic factors, including "river discharge, water use, ground water, lake levels, snow cover, glaciers and ice caps, permafrost and seasonally-frozen ground." It also monitors the reflectivity of the sun's radiation from the earth's surface—called albedo—and various other factors concerning the earth's vegetation, the effects of fire on that vegetation, and soil moisture.

Committee on Earth Observation Satellites, "CEOS EO Handbook—the Important Role of Earth Observations," 2009. www.eohandbook.com.

the earth's climate system. They also intend to better apply this information in sectors of the economy affected the most by weather and climate. They believe this will dominate NOAA research for the next two decades. The agency's Web site explains the potential impact of that focus:

> Imagine a future where we understand and predict climate trends and variability with a reasonable amount of certainty. Armed with this knowledge, we can make informed decisions that reduce the socioeconomic impact of weather events on the ever-increasing global population and help us live in harmony with the delicate checks and balances of nature.[39]

Climate science has already been revolutionized during the past few decades through programs involving scientific observation, research, and analysis of climate change and variability. These data from dozens of sources have been combined into various climate models. Improvements in climate modeling have allowed climatologists to predict and project future climate changes with a high degree of accuracy. However, the NOAA admits that there is still a long way to go:

> While NOAA uses its global climate models to project climate change, uncertainties remain large because of insufficient knowledge about components of the Earth's climate system and the interactions among them. Some biological, geological, and chemical processes in the climate system, long known to be major factors in climate change, remain poorly understood and poorly modeled.[40]

As technology improves, the data collected and used in climate models will also improve, yielding ever-higher accuracy levels in forecasting and prediction.

Better Climate Models

Better climate models will depend on three things: more powerful supercomputers, more observations and measurements, and a better understanding of how climate works. Bigger and better supercomputers will definitely be available. According to William B. Gail, director of strategic development at Microsoft's Virtual Earth, the most powerful supercomputer in 1993 performed 597 gigaflops (597 billion individual mathematical operations) per second. By 2008 supercomputers' processing speed had increased dramatically.

In that year the IBM BlueGene/L supercomputer at California's Lawrence Livermore National Laboratory ran nearly 500 times that many operations (280 teraflops, or 280 trillion individual mathematical operations) per second. Gail predicts that by 2012, supercomputers will be able to perform 10,000 teraflops per second. He explains the importance of those advances, saying they "will let scientists simulate Earth at finer scales and incorporate more realistic physics while keeping the time it takes to run a simulation to a matter of months."[41]

Even with the enormous amount of data currently being collected worldwide, more information is needed if climate models are to reach the level of accuracy needed for future climate change predictions. According to Gavin Schmidt of the Goddard Institute for Space Studies, the scenarios used to construct IPCC's climate models include:

projections for population, technology changes, economic development, resource limitations, and the like for the next few decades to a century. If we consider how much energy people are likely to use, what technology will produce that energy, and combine this information with world population projections, we have an estimate of what emissions will look like in the future. A huge range of issues are built into these scenarios: how quickly the world economy will grow, how much developing countries will progress, what technological breakthroughs will define the twenty-first century, and so on.[42]

It is easy to see that these changes will not be easily converted to numbers and to mathematical formulas. The only thing scientists are able to do for sure is to increase and improve the climate data that is programmable into current and future climate models.

More Observations and Measurements

The NOAA currently measures more than 500 environmental factors that include data from geostationary and polar-orbiting satellites, weather balloons, ships, airplanes, ocean buoys, and submersibles. A geostationary satellite is one that orbits the earth at an elevation of 22,300 miles (35,900km) above the equator. At this altitude the period of rotation for the satellite is equal to the rotation of the earth, keeping the satellite in the same position above the surface. Polar-orbiting satellites called POES (Polar Operational Environmental Satellites) orbit the earth longitudinally, moving around the earth from pole to pole about 14 times each day.

geostationary satellite

A satellite orbiting the earth in such a way as to remain directly above a fixed point on the earth's surface, usually above the equator.

Scientists hope additional observations will come from a new program under development called the Global Earth Observation System of Systems (GEOSS). The NOAA and the intergovernmental Group on Earth Observations, of which the United States is a founding member, are coordinating efforts toward the development of GEOSS. The membership of the Group on Earth Observations as of September 2009 includes 80 individual world governments and the European Commission, the executive branch of the European Union. Also, 56 intergovernmental, international, and regional organizations have become participants in this effort.

The GEOSS will link all current systems and fill the gaps in the measurements being taken, resulting in a more complete picture of the earth's climate and climate changes that occur. The NOAA explains the overall goals of the GEOSS:

> The goal is not simply to "plug the holes" and fill the gaps in current observing systems. Rather, the goal is to coordinate across local and global scales, and among nations, to develop a system that covers the full spectrum of environmental phenomena—from the surface of the sun to the depths of the ocean—and to ensure the various components can speak to and understand each other.[43]

There are thousands of separate data systems in use around the world today, but they do not work together. The GEOSS will hopefully remedy that problem, linking all the systems for the benefit of everyone on earth. According to the NOAA:

> With human ingenuity and the political will of 80 governments, GEOSS is a robust effort dedicated to building an integrated, comprehensive and sustained "system of systems" from many thousands of individual Earth observation technologies around the globe. This essential approach is as integrated as the planet that GEOSS is designed to observe, predict and protect.[44]

To reach these goals and to provide new technology to increase observations worldwide, additions to current technology will be made, including enhanced radar, unmanned aircraft systems, improved buoy systems, and new instrumentation on orbiting satellites.

Phased Array Radar

Doppler radar uses the Doppler effect to produce data about objects at a distance. The Doppler effect can be observed when a vehicle blaring a siren moves past a fixed point—a person standing on a street corner, for example, listening while an ambulance passes by. When the ambulance is approaching, its siren has a certain pitch. As it drives away, that pitch undergoes an obvious change.

Doppler effect

A change in the frequency of light or sound waves as a result of movement either of the source or the receiver of the waves. With sound waves, this effect causes the pitch of the sound to either increase or decrease, depending on whether the source is approaching the receiver or traveling away from it.

Doppler radar takes advantage of that effect. Radar units beam a microwave signal toward a target. The target reflects the signal back to the point of origin. The target alters the signal in the same way sound is altered by the Doppler effect. Analyzing how the original signal has been altered creates an image of the object for the technician sending the microwave signal. Meteorologists use Doppler radar to create images of approaching precipitation, giving them the information they need to predict the speed and direction of the storm.

Currently, Doppler radar is being adapted to include Phased Array Radar (PAR) to locate severe weather. PAR employs multiple beams and frequencies that will reduce the previous data collection time of 5 to 6 minutes to less than 1 minute. This enhanced radar technology could greatly improve the Next Generation Radar (NEXRAD) system for all applications of weather radar. NEXRAD is a network of 158 high-resolution Doppler weather radars that are operated by the National Weather Service.

Phased Array Radar

A radar system using multiple sensors scanning at slightly different frequencies to detect weather phenomena more rapidly.

NEXRAD detects precipitation and wind, processes the data, and displays a map showing patterns of movement that allow weather forecasters to pinpoint storm rotation and better warn citizens of imminent danger from hail, high winds, and tornadoes. Future NEXRADs will have the ability to optically detect the size of hailstones and will pinpoint their location more accurately.

Unmanned Aircraft Systems

Ground-based radars can observe and analyze storms over land, but storms far out over open oceans require other platforms for close observation. Currently, manned NOAA aircraft track hurricanes and even fly into the massive storms, using radar to map their speed and direction. The more detailed data that scientists can gather from these superstorms, the better able they will be to predict their movements in the future, potentially saving thousands of lives in the process. This data will also provide important clues to the overall climate changes that helped create the storms in the first place.

Flying into a hurricane, however, is risky, so the NOAA has begun testing unmanned aircraft that will provide the same data without risking the lives of pilots and crews. In addition to flying into superstorms, there are other locations on earth where manned aircraft cannot safely or economically go, such as areas of ocean that are too far from land and the vast expanses of the frigid Arctic and Antarctic. The NOAA plans to use unmanned, remotely controlled aircraft to collect data from those areas. The data they collect will supplement satellite and ground-based sensors.

This program, called Unmanned Aircraft Systems, has been in use by the military for some years but has only recently been tested for weather and climate observation. When fully implemented, instruments on board these unmanned aircraft will also be used to observe wildlands, volcanic islands, and wildfires—all places where it might be dangerous for manned aircraft to fly. Being able to access more weather and climate data will improve the accuracy of storm forecasting, help assess changes in Arctic ice and its effect on ecosystems, improve flood and drought forecasts, and in general improve scientists' understanding of climate change. The Unmanned Aircraft Systems will be an integral part of the proposed GEOSS.

Updated Buoy Systems

Aircraft, whether manned or unmanned, can collect weather and climate data from the surface to the upper atmosphere, but the earth's climate is also significantly affected by factors beneath the oceans' surfaces—specifically currents, salinity levels, and water temperatures. Scientists currently collect a great deal of data from earth's oceans using vast numbers of buoys, but they are only recently incorporating buoys that can regularly provide information about the oceans' depths. According to the NOAA, improved deep-sea buoys, when employed along with Unmanned Aircraft Systems for atmospheric study, will capture "a vertical profile of conditions from the bottom of the ocean to the top of the atmosphere, and everything in between. This information can lead to improved models of conditions over vast oceans."[45]

The type of buoy recently deployed—Argo buoys, or floats, which were launched between 2000 and 2007—may someday be used for more than reading seawater temperature and salinity. One potential new application for the Argo system is as an early warning system, notifying scientists and governments of seismic disruptions such as tidal waves or tsunamis. With proper technology, they could be programmed to set off smoke signals, flares, flashing lights, or even make automated cell phone calls warning of imminent danger. Another potential use for Argo floats is to monitor levels of nutrients or oxygen in seawater.

A third potential use is for surveillance and security, to report the presence of vessels and divers in areas such as no-dive zones. Finally, the floats could collect data associated with coral reefs and monitor the sounds made by whales and other aquatic animals. Since the data gathered by Argo buoys today and in the future must be transmitted to satellites, those will also need to be improved.

Improvements in Satellite and Computer Technology

For almost 50 years, scientists have relied on climate data gathered by satellites. Every year, the observations and data-collection capabilities of these satellites have increased. There are currently 10 operational weather satellites orbiting earth. Eight of them are in geostationary orbit around the equator. Two of them are in a longitudinal polar orbit. These are only a small fraction of the 800 active satellites currently orbiting the planet.

Scientists agree that obtaining detailed climate information for use in climate models and in determining policy regarding global warming requires the use of increasingly competent satellites. In order to continue observing and recording climate data, many of the aging but active satellites currently in orbit will have to be replaced in the near future. Estimates on the amount of time required to design, build, and launch these replacement satellites range from 5 to 10 years. Consequently, new

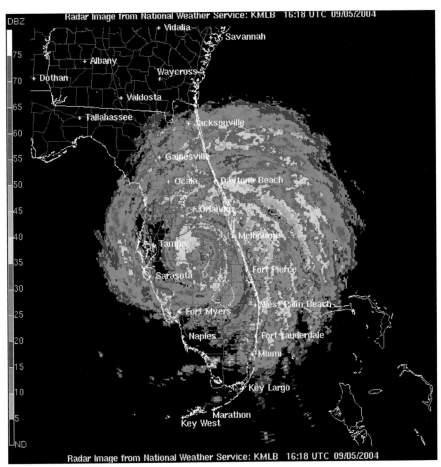

Radar Image from National Weather Service: KMLB 16:18 UTC 09/05/2004

A Doppler radar image shows a very large, very wet Hurricane Frances passing over Florida in 2004. Data on precipitation, wind, and other climatic factors are used to create maps showing patterns of movement of severe storms and other major weather events.

satellites are being planned aggressively to ensure the continuation of observations and measurement of climate change.

Using existing and new technologies and measurement instrumentation, scientists will be able to improve model analysis and test models more accurately against current climate conditions. Also, new models will be able to analyze cloud data to a greater degree, as well as their effect on terrain. Models will also be better able to represent climatic processes occurring within the atmosphere, in the oceans, on landmasses, and out in space. As part of that goal of improving how satellite observations are used, the NOAA plans to combine the data from different modeling systems—to couple them, in other words—to provide a better picture of the earth's climate at any given time. According to the NOAA, "they are working on 'ensemble modeling techniques,' running several models collectively and averaging the results to select the most likely eventuality. The NOAA will be partnering with modeling centers around the world to achieve the most accuracy possible from these ensemble efforts."[46]

New Directions for the Future

On March 19, 2009, President Barack Obama appointed Jane Lubchenco to be the undersecretary of commerce for oceans and atmosphere, as well as the administrator of the NOAA, the nation's top science agency for climate, oceans, and the atmosphere. She is charged with spearheading efforts toward identifying the effects of global warming and with implementing new programs and projects to deal with its effects. When Lubchenco's nomination to the NOAA's highest position was announced, she said: "With hard work and the best science as our guide, NOAA can spur the creation of new jobs and industries, revive our fisheries and the economies and communities they support, improve weather forecasting and disaster warnings, provide credible information about climate change to Americans, and protect and restore our coastal ecosystems."[47]

 SXI Imager

One of the newest satellite instruments developed by the National Oceanic and Atmospheric Administration is the SXI Imager, located on a geostationary satellite above the equator. The SXI Imager relays X-ray images of the sun to scientists on earth virtually in real time. Solar storms can affect power, communication, and navigation systems on earth. By enhancing scientists' ability to detect new solar storms, SXI Imagers also enhance their ability to predict climate effects on earth that are linked to those storms.

Three SXI satellites have been launched: the first, GOES-12 SXI, on July 23, 2001; the second, GOES-13 SXI, on May 24, 2006; and the third, GOES-14 SXI, on June 27, 2009. These SXI Imagers are among the new generation of climate observation satellites, leading the way into the climate research of the future.

Lubchenco represented the United States at the December 2009 UN Climate Change Conference in Copenhagen, Denmark. Representatives from 170 countries, numerous nongovernmental organizations, and countless journalists were in attendance—a total of 8,000 people.

According to the Copenhagen Climate Council, the six goals of the international summit on climate change were:

1. Agreement on a science-based greenhouse gas stabilization path with 2020 and 2050 emissions reduction targets that will achieve it;

2. Effective measurement, reporting and verification of emissions performance by business;

3. Incentives for a dramatic increase in financing low emissions technology;

4. Deployment of existing low-emissions technologies and the development of new ones;

5. Funds to make communities more resilient and able to adapt to the effects of climate change, and

6. Means to finance forest protection.[48]

Unfortunately, the conference, known as COP 15 (Conference of the Parties, Fifteenth Session), did not accomplish all its goals. World leaders were frustrated with its limited success and with the less-than-ambitious progress indicated by the Copenhagen Accord, the document issued at the end of the conference. Still, most called COP 15 a significant first step, with the next conference, COP 16, scheduled for Mexico City on November 29, 2010.

Despite the world's disappointment with COP 15, some believed the meeting accomplished some good. David Doniger, a policy director of the Natural Resources Defense Council, an environmental group headquartered in New York, felt that the Copenhagen Accord

> broke through years of negotiating gridlock to achieve three critical goals. First, it provides for real cuts in heat-trapped carbon pollution by all of the world's big emitters. Second, it establishes a transparent framework for evaluating countries' performance against their commitments. And third, it will start an

unprecedented flow of resources to help poor and vulnerable nations cope with climate impacts, protect their forests and adopt clean energy technologies.[49]

It remains to be seen what the long-term benefits of the Copenhagen Accord will be. The ongoing measurement of climate change will continue. How these measurements are used and what changes will be made in greenhouse gas emissions will be up to the leaders of the world. Hopefully, they will take steps to ensure the continued livability of earth's climate for generations to come.

Source Notes

Introduction: Science in Action

1. Quoted in Mark Lynas, *Six Degrees: Our Future on a Hotter Planet.* Washington, DC: National Geographic Society, 2008, p. 133.

2. Lynas, *Six Degrees*, p. 133.

Chapter One: What Is Climate Change?

3. Shishmaref Erosion & Relocation Coalition, "We Are Worth Saving." www.shishmarefrelocation.com.

4. Gavin Schmidt and Joshua Wolfe, *Climate Change: Picturing the Science.* New York: Norton, 2009, p. 1.

5. Quoted in Schmidt and Wolfe, *Climate Change*, 2009, p. 135.

6. Cartographic Division, "The Earth's Fractured Surface," map supplement, *National Geographic*, April 1995.

7. Jason Wolfe, "Volcanoes & Climate Change," NASA Earth Observatory, September 5, 2000. http://earthobservatory.nasa.gov.

8. Quoted in Wolfe, "Volcanoes & Climate Change."

9. Tom O'Neill, "Changing Climate," map supplement, *National Geographic*, October 2007.

10. Quoted in Noel Wanner, "Sunspots: The Effects of Sunspots on the Earth's Climate," Exploratorium, 1998. www.exploratorium.edu.

11. Quoted in Schmidt and Wolfe, *Climate Change*, p. 137.

Chapter Two: Reading Climate Change in the Earth

12. Stephen K. Ewings, "Measuring Climate Change," Global Warming, Climate Change, Greenhouse Effect, 2007. www.global-greenhouse-warming.com.

13. European Space Agency, "ESA Investigates New Methods of Mapping Tropical Forest from Space," August 21, 2009. www.esa.int.

14. Keith Briffa, "Trees as Indicators of Climate Change," Lustia Dendrochronology Project, January 1, 2004. http://lustiag.pp.fi.

15. Virginia Morell, "Signs from Earth: Now What?" *National Geographic*, September 2004. http://environment.nationalgeographic. com.

16. Quoted in Gerard Wynn, "Two Meter Sea Level Rise Unstoppable: Experts," Reuters, September 30, 2009. www.reuters.com.

17. Quoted in Wynn, "Two Meter Sea Level Rise Unstoppable."

18. Ewings, "Measuring Climate Change."

Chapter Three: Temperature and Precipitation

19. Public Broadcasting System and the WGBH Educational Foundation, *Surviving the Dust Bowl,* broadcast November 16, 2009. www.pbs.org.

20. Quoted in Public Broadcasting System and the WGBH Educational Foundation, *Surviving the Dust Bowl.*

21. NASA, "ER-2 Aircraft Program," June 30, 2005. www.nasa.gov.

22. "The Rationale Behind Argo," Argo Project Office, February 2006. http://argo.jcommops.org.

23. Priit J.Vesilind, "The Driest Place on Earth," *National Geographic*, August 2003. http://ngm.nationalgeographic.com.

24. Laura Allen, "Endangered Orbits," *Popular Science*, August 2007, pp. 64–65.

25. Sarah DeWitt, "NASA Global Precipitation Measurement Mission Passes Major Review," NASA's Goddard Space Flight Center, December 8, 2009. www.nasa.gov.

26. Quoted in DeWitt, "NASA Global Precipitation Measurement Mission Passes Major Review."

Chapter Four: Climate Models

27. Lynas, *Six Degrees*, pp. 135–36.

28. Quoted in Carl Zimmer, "The El Niño Factor," *Discover*, January 1999, pp. 101–2.

29. Environmental Protection Agency, "Climate Change: How Do Scientists Predict Future Climate Change?" April 22, 2009. www.epa. gov.

30. Maria Setzer, "Understanding Climate Through Modeling," NOAA, November 2, 2007. http://celebrating200years.noaa.gov.

31. NOAA, "The First Climate Model," 2007. http://celebrating 200years.noaa.gov.

32. NOAA, "The First Climate Model."

33. Setzer, "Understanding Climate Through Modeling."

34. Lynas, *Six Degrees*, p. 151.

35. Quoted in *Science Daily*, "Climate Models Look Good When Predicting Climate Change," April 6, 2008. www.sciencedaily.com.

36. *Science Daily*, "Climate Models Look Good When Predicting Climate Change."

37. Quoted in *Science Daily*, "New Study Increases Concerns About Climate Model Reliability," December 12, 2007. www.sciencedaily. com.

Chapter Five: Climate Technology of the Future

38. Committee on Earth Observation Satellites, "CEOS EO Handbook—the Important Role of Earth Observations," 2009. www.eo handbook.com.

39. NOAA, "The Future of Climate Research," April 25, 2007. http:// celebrating200years.noaa.gov.

40. NOAA, "The Future of Climate Research."

41. William B. Gail, "Climate Control," Discovery Channel, April 13, 2009. http://dsc.discovery.com.

42. Schmidt and Wolfe, *Climate Change*, p. 198.

43. NOAA, "More Observations + Better Models = Faster Warnings, More Accurate Tracking, Improved Forecasts," November 2, 2007. http://celebrating200years.noaa.gov.

44. NOAA, "Earth as a New Frontier: The World-Changing Capability of the Global Earth Observation System of Systems (GEOSS)," 2009. www.noaa.gov.

45. NOAA, "More Observations + Better Models = Faster Warnings, More Accurate Tracking, Improved Forecasts."

46. NOAA, "More Observations + Better Models = Faster Warnings, More Accurate Tracking, Improved Forecasts."

47. NOAA, "Jane Lubchenco Confirmed as NOAA Administrator," March 19, 2009. www.noaanews.noaa.gov.

48. Sara Pickering, "Business 'Call' Outlines Six Steps for Ambitious Global Climate Treaty," Copenhagen Climate Council, May 26, 2009. www.copenhagenclimatecouncil.com.

49. Quoted in Tom Zeller Jr., "Fault Lines Remain After Climate Talks," *New York Times*, January 3, 2010. http://www.nytimes.com.

Facts About Climate Change

Signs of Global Warming

- There are three essential numbers related to global warming: 280, 385, and 350. Until about 1850, earth's atmosphere contained 280 parts per million (ppm) of carbon dioxide. Today it contains 385 ppm. Leading scientists feel 350 ppm is the highest safe level for living things on earth.
- The average global temperature has climbed 1.4°F (0.8°C) since the late 1800s. Scientists estimate the average temperature will rise an additional 2.5 to 10.4°F (1.4° to 5.8°C) by 2100.
- The first decade of the twenty-first century was the hottest in 400 years. The 10 warmest years on record world-wide (as of 2010) occurred between 1998 and 2009.
- On September 12, 2008, the average minimum coverage of Arctic sea ice dropped to 1.74 million square miles (4.52 million sq. km). This was 860,000 square miles (2.24 million sq. km) below the 1979 to 2000 average minimum.
- Montana's Glacier National Park has only 26 glaciers now, and all of them are shrinking in size. In 1850, at the end of the Little Ice Age, there were 150.
- In 1998, the forth-hottest year on record (as of 2010), 16 percent of all coral reefs died from warmer ocean temperatures.
- The number of Category 4 and 5 hurricanes has doubled over the past 30 years. A record of four Category 5 hurricanes formed in 2005. In 2007 two Category 5 hurricanes made landfall in Central America, another seasonal record.

Effects of Climate Change in the Twenty-First Century

- Greenhouse gases remain in the atmosphere for a long time, so even if emissions ceased today, global warming would continue for decades.

- Sea levels could rise as much as 3.3 to 6.6 feet (1 to 2 m) by the end of the twenty-first century, depending on how much Arctic and Antarctic ice melts and adds water to the oceans.
- The Greenland ice cap, should it completely melt, contains enough water to raise global sea levels by 23 feet (7m). Average global temperatures 125,000 years ago were about 0.56°F (1°C) higher than they are now. Sea levels during that time were 16 to 20 feet (5 to 6 m) higher than they are now. Scientists have determined that melting of the Greenland ice sheet caused most of that increase.
- The West Antarctic ice sheet holds about 500,000 cubic miles (2.2 million cu. km) of ice—about the same amount of ice as in the Greenland ice sheet. The Intergovernmental Panel on Climate Change report of 2007 estimated that a full collapse of the Antarctic ice sheet would raise sea levels by 16 feet (5m) globally.

Carbon Dioxide Emissions

- In 2007, according to the Environmental Protection Agency, U.S. emissions of carbon dioxide were 20.2 percent higher than those in 1990.
- A report from the Netherlands Environmental Assessment Agency states that China's emission of carbon dioxide increased by 8 percent in 2007, accounting for two-thirds of the growth in the year's global greenhouse gas emissions and surpassing the United States' 7 percent growth that year.
- The United States leads the world in carbon dioxide emissions *per person*. The average American is responsible for approximately 19.4 tons (17.6 metric tons) per year. The average Russian is responsible for 11.8 tons (10.7 metric tons). The average citizens of the European Union, China, and India are responsible for 8.6 tons (7.8 metric tons), 5.1 tons (4.6 metric tons), and 1.8 tons (1.6 metric tons), respectively.

Methane Emissions

- Methane has 21 times as much warming effect on the atmosphere as carbon dioxide does.

- Cattle contribute 71 percent of all animal-produced methane emissions to the atmosphere.
- A cow can produce between 8.8 and 17.7 cubic feet (250 to 500 L) of methane per day. This is roughly the volume of a crate that would hold a student's school desk.
- When cattle are fed higher-quality feeds such as alfalfa, they produce less methane.

Related Organizations

Center for the Study of Carbon Dioxide and Global Change
PO Box 25697
Tempe, AZ 85285-5697
phone: (480) 966-3719
Web site: www.co2science.org

The Center for the Study of Carbon Dioxide and Global Change publishes a weekly online magazine, *CO₂ Science*, with editorials and reviews of current publications, including scientific journals, books, and other educational materials. The group's stated goal is to separate fantasy from reality in the climate change debate.

The Climate Project
2100 West End Ave., Suite 600
Nashville, TN 37203
phone: (615) 327-7577
e-mail: info@theclimateproject.org
Web site: www.theclimateproject.org

The Climate Project is a nonprofit organization that consists of more than 3,000 diverse and dedicated volunteers worldwide who have been personally trained by former U.S. vice president and Nobel laureate Al Gore to educate the public and to raise awareness about climate change.

The Earth Lab Foundation
625 Fourth Ave., #200
Kirkland, WA 98033
phone: (425) 284-4265
fax: (425) 294-4266
e-mail: info@earthlab.com
Web site: www.earthlabfoundation.org

The Earth Lab foundation is a nonprofit organization that provides research and education that promotes clean-energy technologies. They provide online calculators to help individuals determine their carbon footprint—how environmentally friendly their lifestyle is.

National Aeronautics and Space Administration (NASA)

Public Communications Office

NASA Headquarters

Suite 5K39

Washington, DC 20546-0001

phone: (202) 358-0001

fax: (202) 358-4338

Web site: www.nasa.gov

NASA is the United States' space agency. In addition to launching manned and unmanned space vehicles, NASA also helps monitor environmental factors using its satellite technology.

National Oceanic and Atmospheric Administration (NOAA)

1401 Constitution Ave. NW, Room 5128

Washington, DC 20230

phone: (301) 713-1208

Web site: www.noaa.gov

The NOAA is a scientific agency within the U.S. Department of Commerce, that focuses on conditions of the oceans and the atmosphere. The NOAA issues weather warnings, charts seas and skies, and provides guidance in the use of ocean and coastal resources.

The Pew Center on Global Climate Change

2101 Wilson Blvd., Suite 550

Arlington, VA 22201

phone: (703) 516-4146

fax: (703) 841-1422

Web site: www.pewclimate.org

The Pew Center on Global Climate Change is a nonprofit, nonpartisan organization whose goal is to provide credible information about and innovative solutions for the world's environmental issues. The Pew Center brings together business leaders, policy makers, scientists, and other experts to provide a forum for objective research and analysis of climate change.

Science and Environmental Policy Project (SEPP)

1600 S. Eads St., Suite 712-S
Arlington, VA 22202-2907
phone/fax: (703) 920-2744
e-mail: comments@sepp.org
Web site: www.sepp.org

SEPP was founded by physicist S. Fred Singer to encourage scientifically sound, cost-effective decisions on health and the environment. The group challenges the climate change research findings and conclusions of many international scientific organizations and promotes the theory of climate change based on natural causes.

The Sierra Club

85 Second St., 2nd Floor
San Francisco, CA 94105
phone: (415) 977-5500
fax: (415) 977-5799
e-mail: information@sierraclub.org
Web site: www.sierraclub.org

Since 1892 the Sierra Club has been the largest grassroots environmental organization in the United States. It works to protect communities, wild places, and the planet itself by promoting the responsible use of the earth's resources.

Union of Concerned Scientists (UCS)

Two Brattle Square
Cambridge, MA 02238-9105
phone: (617) 547-5552
fax: (617) 864-9405
Web site: www.ucsusa.org

The Union of Concerned Scientists is an independent, science-based organization composed of citizens and scientists who work to promote a healthy environment and a safe world. In addition to climate change, the group has programs focused on clean air and water, and other environmental concerns.

For Further Research

Books

David Archer, *The Long Thaw: How Humans Are Changing the Next 100,000 Years of Earth's Climate*. Princeton, NJ: Princeton University Press, 2009.

Kirstin Dow and Thomas E. Downing, *The Atlas of Climate Change: Mapping the World's Greatest Challenge*. Berkeley and Los Angeles: University of California Press, 2007.

Al Gore, *An Inconvenient Truth: The Planetary Emergency of Global Warming and What We Can Do About It*. New York: Rodale, 2006.

Mark Lynas, *Six Degrees: Our Future on a Hotter Planet*. Washington DC: National Geographic Society, 2008.

Gavin Schmidt and Joshua Wolfe, *Climate Change: Picturing the Science*. New York: Norton, 2009.

Web Sites

Climate Change, Environmental Protection Agency (www.epa.gov/climatechange). The Environmental Protection Agency's Climate Change site offers comprehensive information on the issue of climate change in a way that is accessible and meaningful to all parts of society—communities, individuals, businesses, states and localities, and governments.

Exploratorium (www.exploratorium.edu). At this Web site, students can explore scientific data relating to the atmosphere, the oceans, the areas covered by ice and snow, and the living organisms in all these domains. Students will also get a sense of how scientists study natural phenomena—how researchers gather evidence, test theories, and come to conclusions.

The Nature Conservancy: Climate Change (www.nature.org/initiatives/climatechange). Information on how climate change affects wildlife.

New Scientist: Climate Change (www.newscientist.com/topic/climate-change). What is climate change, how do we know it is happening, and what can we expect? Students can delve into it with this beginner's guide.

NOAA Earth Handbook (http://celebrating200years.noaa.gov/edufun/book/welcome.html). A handbook for students about the earth and the NOAA.

On Being a Scientist: A Guide to Responsible Conduct in Research (www.nap.edu/openbook.php?record_id=12192&page=R1). This is a free, downloadable book from the National Academy of Sciences Committee on Science, Engineering, and Public Policy. The 2009 edition provides a clear explanation of the responsible conduct of scientific research. Chapters on treatment of data, mistakes and negligence, the scientist's role in society, and other topics offer invaluable insight for student researchers.

Pew Climate Change 101 (www.pewclimate.org/docUploads/Climate 101-Complete-Jan09.pdf). A primer for basic information on all aspects of climate change.

United Nations Environment Programme: Pachamama (www.grida.no/publications/other/geo2000/pacha). The kids' section of the United Nations site provides information on a wide range of issues related to the environment.

World Wildlife Fund: Climate (www.worldwildlife.org/climate). Students can learn about the World Wildlife Fund Climate Program and what they can do to make a difference.

Index

absolute desert, 47
aircraft
  ER-2, 44
  unmanned, 71, 72
air temperature, measuring,
  42–44
Alaska, 15, 16 (illustration)
Allen, Laura, 50
altimetry, defined, 29
Anglo-Saxon Chronicle, 26
Antarctica
  climate, 10
  ice core data, 38, 39, 39
    (illustration)
anthrogenic, defined, 58
Arctic
  climate, 10
  climate model simulations for,
    60
  melting ice caps, 36
  tree rings north of Circle, 33
Argo, 44–45
Argo buoys/floats, 72
Atacama Desert, 46 (illustration),
  47
Australia, 36

Barnosky, Tony, 55
beech trees, 10
Bennike, Ole, 10
biomass, 29, 30–32
BIOMASS mission, 32
biosphere, defined, 17
Black Sea, 31

Briffa, Keith, 32–33
bristlecone pines, 33
buoy systems, 71–72

calcium carbonate skeletons, 35
Canada, 10–11
Cane, Mark, 54
carbon dioxide (CO_2), 11, 38
Carrasco, Marc, 55
climate
  defined, 15–17
  essential variables, 66, 67
  human influences on. *See*
    greenhouse gases
  natural influences on, 17
    earth's orbit and axial tilt, 22,
      23
    plate tectonics, 17–21, 19
      (illustration)
    solar radiation, 22–24
    volcanic eruptions, 18–
      20, 21 (illustration),
      25 (illustration), 61
      (illustration)
climate models
  accuracy, 59, 62–63
  computers and, 55–56
  coupled, 62
  creation of improved, 64,
    67–68, 73–74
  current, 58–59
  data manipulation, 60
  defined, 54
  ensemble techniques, 74

first, 56–58
purpose of, 13–14, 54–55, 56
climatologist, defined, 10
Clouds and the Earth's Radiant
  Energy System, 50
Coen, Floyd, 41–42
Committee on Earth Observation
  Satellites (CEOS), 64
computers
  climate models and, 55–56
  importance of, 57–58
  supercomputers, 13, 67
Conference of the Parties,
  Fifteenth Session (COP 15), 75
Copenhagen Accord, 75–76
Copenhagen Climate Council, 75
coral rings, 34–36, 37
coupled climate models, 62
cryosphere, defined, 56

data, importance of, 13
data collection methods. *See*
  measurement methods
data loggers, 42
dendrochronology, 32–33, 33
  (illustration)
Denkinger, Judith, 37
desertification, defined, 30
DeWitt, Sarah, 51
disdrometers, 48
disease, 53
Doniger, David, 75–76
Doppler effect, defined, 70
Doppler radar, 49, 70, 73
  (illustration)
Dual-Frequency Precipitation
  Radar, 51
Dust Bowl, 41–42, 42
  (illustration)

dust pneumonia, 41

Earth Explorer satellite, 32
earth's orbit and axial tilt
  fluctuations, 22, 23
East Africa, 53
eccentricity (of earth's orbit), 23
Electronic Maximum-Minimum
  Temperature Sensor (MMTS),
  42
Ellesmere Island fossils, 10–11
El Niño, 53–54, 57 (illustration)
Enhanced Vegetation Index, 30
ensemble modeling techniques, 74
ER-2 aircraft, 44
European Space Agency, 31–32
evaporation, 47
Ewings, Stephen K., 29; 38
extinction of species, 37

Fischer, George, 24
Flexible Modeling System, 58
floats, 44–45
the flood (Noah's), 31
fossils from Pliocene epoch,
  10–11
Francis, Jane, 10
Frelich, Michael, 51

Gail, William B., 67
Galapagos, 37
Galileo Galilei, 42
general-circulation models, 56
Geophysical Fluid Dynamics
  Laboratory (GFDL), 56, 57
Geostationary Operational
  Environmental satellites, 50
geostationary satellites, 50, 68,
  74

Global Climate Observing System (GCOS), 66
Global Earth Observation System (GEOSS), 68–69, 71
global geography, 10
Global Precipitation Measurement (GPM) Project, 50–51
global warming
    defined, 17, 27
    effect of carbon dioxide on, 11
    scientists' view of, 13, 27
Global Warming: What You Can Do (Ewings), 29
GPM Microwave Imager, 51
greenhouse effect, 25–27
greenhouse gases
    defined, 13
    human responsibility for, 13, 24, 27
    increase in emission of, 27
    primary types of, 25
    sun and, 25–26
Greenland ice core data, 39
Group on Earth Observations, 69

Hall, Tim, 17, 26
Harington, Richard, 10–11
Hawaii, 45, 47
Haywood, Alan, 11
hot towers, 50
hurricane Rita, 50
hurricanes, 50, 71
hydrosphere, defined, 56

IBM BlueGene/L supercomputers, 67
ice cap melting, 36
ice cores, 38–39, 39 (illustration)

illness, 53
imaging methods, 49
Indonesia, 19
Industrial Revolution, 27
infrared radiation, 22, 25–26
instruments. *See* measurement methods

Jason-1 satellite, 36
Jason-2 satellite, 36–37

Lightning Imaging Sensor, 50
Little Ice Age, 24, 26, 27
Little Lake, Oregon, 34
livestock raising, 24
Lubchenco, Jane, 74–75
luminosity of sun, 24
Lynas, Mark
    on carbon dioxide levels during Pliocene, 11
    on El Niño, 53–54
    on limitations of climate models, 59
    on model simulations for Arctic, 60

magnetic fields on sun, 24
measurement methods, 11, 29
    aircraft, 44, 71
    buoy systems, 71–72
    coral rings, 34–36, 37
    disdrometers, 48
    floats, 44–45
    ice cores, 38–39, 39 (illustration)
    MMTS, 42
    radar, 49, 70, 73 (illustration)
    radiosondes, 43, 44
    rain gauges, 45, 47–48

sediment layers, 34, 35
(illustration)
thermometers, 42
tree rings, 32–33, 33
(illustration)
weather radar, 48–49
See also satellites
Mediterranean Sea, 31
Microwave Imager, 50
Milankovitch, Milutin, 23
Milankovitch cycles, 23
Miocene Mammal Mapping
Project (MIOMAP), 55
MODIS (Moderate Resolution
Imaging Spectroradiometer),
30–31
Morell, Virginia, 34
mosquitoes, 53
Mount Pinatubo eruption
(Philippines), 19–20, 25
(illustration), 61 (illustration)
Mount Waialeale, Hawaii, 45, 47
Munjong (crown prince of Korea),
45

National Aeronautics and Space
Administration (NASA)
ER-2 aircraft, 44
MODIS, 30–31
sensor web satellites, 44
TRMM, 49–50
National Geographic (magazine),
18, 22, 34, 47
National Oceanic and
Atmospheric Administration
(NOAA)
current administrator, 74
GEOSS, 69
GFDL, 56, 57

improved climate model
development, 73–74
plan for future, 65–67
SXI Imagers, 74
Unmanned Aircraft Systems
and, 71
National Space Development
Agency (NASDA, Japan),
49–50
National Weather Service, 70
Next Generation Radar
(NEXRAD), 70
Noah's flood, 31

Obama, Barack, 74
O'Neill, Tom, 22

paleoclimatologist, defined, 10, 11
particulates, 18–20, 21
(illustration)
permafrost, 15, 16 (illustration)
Peru, 57 (illustration)
Phased Array Radar (PAR), 70
Philippines, 19–20, 25
(illustration), 61 (illustration)
photosphere, 22, 23–24
Pitman, Walter, 31
plate tectonics, 17–21, 19
(illustration)
Pliocene epoch, 10–11
Polar-Orbiting Environmental
Satellites (POES), 50, 68
Popular Science (magazine), 50
Porites corals, 36
precession (of earth), 23
precipitation
during Dust Bowl, 41–42
effects of higher than usual, 53,
57 (illustration)

measuring, 45, 46 (illustration),
    47–51, 70–71, 73
    (illustration)
rainfall changes, 51
tree rings and, 32
Precipitation Radar, 49–50

radar, 48–49, 70, 73 (illustration)
radiation from sun
    Milankovitch cycles and, 23
    sunspots effect on, 22–24
    types of, 22
radio-meteorograph, 43
radiosondes, 43, 44
Rahmstorf, Stefan, 37–38
rain. *See* precipitation
rain gauges, 45, 47–48
rain shadow, defined, 47
Rapid Response System, 30
reference radiosondes, 43
Reichler, Thomas, 62
Rift Valley fever, 53
Ryan, William, 31

satellites, 12 (illustration)
    geostationary, 50, 68, 74
    imaging methods, 49–51
    improvements in data-
        collectioon capabilities, 72–73
    to measure air temperature, 44
    to measure biomass, 30–32
    to measure rainfall, 48–51
    to measure sea levels, 36–37
    to measure storms on sun, 74
    polar-orbiting, 50, 68
    to transmit data, 42
Schmidt, Gavin, 16–17, 68
Science Daily (magazine), 62–63
sea level changes, 29, 36–38

seawater temperatures
    coral rings and, 35
    measuring, 44–45, 71–72
sediment layers, 34
Sejong (king of Korea), 45
Sethi, 31–32
Setzer, Maria, 56, 60
Shishmaref, Alaska, 15, 16
    (illustration)
Singer, Fred S., 63
*Six Degrees: Our Future on a
    Hotter Planet* (Lynas), 11, 53
Smagorinsky, Joseph, 57–58
solar maximum (solar max), 24
solar minimum (solar min), 24
Special Sensor Microwave Imager,
    50
species extinction, 37
stratosphere, defined, 20
sun
    greenhouse gases and, 25–26
    radiation from, 22–24
    storms on, 74
    volcanic eruptions and, 18–19
    X-ray images of, 74
sunspots, 22–24
supercomputers, 13, 67
Surviving the Dust Bowl (television
    documentary), 41
SXI Imagers, 74

Tambora eruption (Indonesia), 19
tectonic plates, 17–21, 19
    (illustration)
Tedford, Richard, 10–11
temperatures
    during Dust Bowl, 41
    evaporation and, 47
    measuring air, 42–44

measuring seawater, 44–45, 71–72

during Pliocene, 11

rainfall and, 51

of sea and coral rings, 35

winter, after Pinatubo eruption, 20

thermometers, 42

Tin Creek, Alaska, 15

tipping buckets, 48

TOPEX/Poseiden satellite, 36

tornadoes, 65 (illustration)

tree line, 10

tree rings, 32–33, 33 (illustration)

tropical forests, 31–32

tropical rainfall, measuring, 49–50

Tropical Rainfall Measuring Mission (TRMM), 49–50

Tropisar, 31–32

ultraviolet light, defined, 22

UN Climate Change Conference, 75

Univac 1108, 58

Unmanned Aircraft Systems, 71, 72

varves, 34, 35 (illustration)

vegetation patterns, 30

Vellinga, Pier, 38

Vesilind, Priit J., 47

Visible and Infrared Scanner, 50

visible light, defined, 22

volcanic eruptions
effect on climate, 18–19
examples of, 19–20, 21 (illustration), 25 (illustration), 61 (illustration)

weather, defined, 15

weather radar, 48–49

Whitlock, Cathy, 34

Wolfe, Jason, 20

X-ray images of sun, 74

"year without a summer," 19

Zebiak, Stephen, 54

Picture Credits

Cover: iStockphoto.com
AP Images: 16, 57, 61, 73
iStockphoto.com: 9 (top), 12
Photos.com: 8, 9 (bottom), 65
Science Photo Library: 19, 21, 25, 33, 35, 39, 43, 46

About the Authors

Charles and Linda George have authored dozens of nonfiction books for children and teens on a wide variety of topics including world religions, ancient civilizations, Native Americans, the civil rights movement, plate tectonics, gene therapy, Alcatraz, and the Holocaust. Charles taught secondary Spanish, history, and math, and Linda taught in the elementary grades before they "retired" from teaching to write full-time. They live in a small town in west Texas.

ABOUT THE AUTHORS